EDITED BY
GORDANA NIKOLIĆ
& ŠEFIK TATLIĆ
# THE GRAY ZONES OF CREATIVITY & CAPITAL

Theory on Demand #17

The Gray Zones of Creativity and Capital

Editors: Šefik Tatlić, Gordana Nikolić
Copy-editing: Josip Batinić, Inte Gloerich, Léna Robin, Nina Živančević
Editorial Support: Miriam Rasch
Translation: Novica Petrović (for 'The Art of New Class Geography of the City')

Design: Josip Batinić, Léna Robin
EPUB development: Josip Batinić, Léna Robin
Printer: 'Print on Demand'
Publisher: Institute of Network Cultures, Amsterdam 2015
ISBN: 978-94-92302-03-8

Contact
Institute of Network Cultures
Phone: +31 20 5951865
Email: info@networkcultures.org
Web: http://www.networkcultures.org

This publication is available through various print on demand services.
EPUB and PDF editions of this publication are freely downloadable from
our website, http://www.networkcultures.org/publications/#tods

Institute of
network cultures

CONTENTS

THE GRAY ZONES OF CREATIVITY AND CAPITAL: INTRODUCTION

ŠEFIK TATLIĆ AND GORDANA NIKOLIĆ

The initial idea that led to the preparation of this publication was not a reflection of the editors' wish to merely add another publication focusing on a critique of the relationship between creative industries and capital to the huge corpus of similar publications taking a critical stance towards the process of co-optation of creativity, creative industries, art or the domain of abstraction in general by capital. Even though, precisely through the logic of the mass production of critical texts dealing with the above-mentioned context, this publication as well will ultimately exist in such a register, the distinctive feature of this publication is its aspiration to place the relationship between creativity and capital in the context of an analysis wherein capitalism is treated as the framework of a broader relationship of domination, which to a great degree goes beyond the currently popular critical niche focused on analyzing the relationship between creativity, abstraction or representation in general and capital.

The vast majority of such publications are characterized by such a perception of the relationship between creativity and capital, which implies that the co-optation and exploitation of work, creativity and attention occurs in a post-class, post-ideological or post-colonial context of the so-called 'networked world or networked democracy', wherein all subjects and their actions are reportedly subjected to the logic of capital in the same way. Regardless of whether we speak of the ideological use of the concept of creativity in the name of rationalization of the neoliberal strategies of transforming the city into ghettoized class and racial apartheids, whether we speak of the exploitation of attention (the economy of attention) by financial capital or generally about the episte-mological positioning of creativity, abstraction or the domain of representation within the dominant form of rationalization and reproduction of capitalism, this publication strives to retain a critical view that sees these processes as forms of the perpetuation of the hegemony of capitalism in the so-called contemporary era.

As regards the temporal framework encompassed in this publication, although certain texts, through the logic of the necessity of historicization of specific strategies and practices refer to historical periods preceding the 21st century, the majority of the texts contained in this publication refer to social and political processes from the end of the 20th and the beginning of the 21st century, that is, the current period. In this sense, the dominant ideological discourses, strategies and power relations of today constitute the focus of attention of the topics of this publication.

This publication, then, occupies a position that treats 'the networked world', its democ-racies, cognitivities, attention and culture as domains wherein, or with help of which, forms of the reproduction of capitalism as a heterogeneous form of hegemony, primarily of the First World of capital or the West, are reorganized, 'modernized'. The title 'The Gray Zones of Creativity and Capital' does not, therefore, point primarily to instances of vagueness and dichotomy in the analysis of the social meaning of the cooperation between creativity and capital, but assumes a critical stance towards 'gray areas' in those dominant interpretations of capitalism that try to view it as a post-ideological, post-class or post-bloc system.

Before shortly introducing the texts it should be noted that this publication in its iteration in Serbian language contained one article that is not featured in this English iteration. The text had to be left out because of copyright contraints that don't allow this text to be featured in an online publication. The text in question was written by Santiago Castro-Gómez and it is entitled 'The Missing Chapter of Empire—Postmodern reorganization of coloniality and post-Fordist capitalism' (*Cultural Studies Volume 21*, Issue 2-3, 2007).[1] This text, by critically refering to the book *Empire* by Antonio Negri and Michael Hardt, criticized the view of capitalism as a system of equal exploitation of all. Castro-Gómez saw the capitalism of today as a modernized form of the colonial division of the world, in which the First World of capital, the West, still retains a monopoly on defining progress, and in which that same world retains a surplus of privileges within the framework of the unbalanced distribution of global wealth. This text's role was to position this publica-tion in decolonial register which is still the register in which this publication continues to reside.

The text by Jonathan Beller entitled 'Within the Image' analyses in a similar manner, but from a different perspective, the socio-political meaning and the ideological effects of the capitalist exploitation of the image and attention. From a structuralist position, Beller analyses the role which the commodification of the image, attention and abstraction plays in the neoliberal free market and its ideologies, but in those same contemporary forms of capitalism the author also detects a specific colonial and racial relationship of domination.

Josephine Berry Slater's text 'Neutralizing Engaged Subjects in the Creative City', relying on Foucault's theoretical apparatus, criticizes the biopolitical and repressive character of the neoliberal strategies of transforming urban Great Britain in the post-Thatcher era. Even though Slater locates the roots of the neoliberal strategies of social engineering and the *laissez-faire* concept of organizing society and the economy in Thatcher's attack on the role of society in the regulation of society, the author links the roots of the deroga-tion of subversive social engagement with the contemporary forms of organization of capitalism, in an alliance with the modern art mainstream.

---

1   http://www.tandfonline.com/doi/abs/10.1080/09502380601162639

Marc James Léger's text 'The Agency of Art in the Unconscious' critically addresses contemporary art as a form of reproducing the nullity of social significance contained in the domain of creativity in capitalism. Relying to a large extent on the psychoanalytic theories of Lacan and Žižek, Leger structurally links contemporary art and the domain of creativity in general to modern political economy a way that sees contemporary art as a form of neutralization of radical fiction that antagonizes the above-mentioned relationship with capitalist economy.

'The Art of New Class Geography of the City—Culture-guided urban regeneration serving the modernization of the periphery' is a text by Ana Vilenica wherein she critically addresses the practices and principles contained in the neoliberal establishment of a class geography of urban environments in Serbia. Vilenica's text does not remain at the level of analyzing the neoliberal strategies of contemporary capitalism, but also deals with the broader meaning of class and racial principles invested in the processes of modernization in general. In this sense, Vilenica analyzes the effects of an alliance of sorts between capital and creative industries, emphasizing the role of art and culture in contemporary capitalist ideological rhetorics.

Sandi Abram's text 'The Creative Factory: Collective Creativity and Autonomy in the Neoliberal Machine of Creative Industries' analyzes the effects of post-Fordist cognitive capitalism on the social scene in Ljubljana, Slovenia. Abram assumes a critical stance towards the public-private partnership model invested in the processes of producing a new class geography of urban environments, which is a model that Abram sees as a part of a broader pan-European paradigm of gentrification. Analyzing the transformation of the Rog factory in Ljubljana, Abram sees the processes of gentrification as parts of a broader capitalist strategy of turning the entire society into a factory and/or a specific commodified niche in the hierarchies of capitalist exploitation.

The text by Irmgard Emmelheinz, entitled 'Neoliberalism and the Autonomy of Art: The Culture of Power, the Power of Culture' analyses the effects of reconfiguring the social-political role of the figure of 'the Other' in the context of Mexico and/or the broader region of Latin America. Emmelheinz takes a critical position in relation to postmodern democratic culture and the institutions of contemporary art than she sees to be a part of the broader process of the utilization of culture by capitalism. The author concludes that within the space of division of political and aesthetic representation occurs a paradigmatic change in the role of culture in neoliberal capitalism, whose autonomy no longer points to its ability to produce a radical criticism of the system, but precisely the opposite -to its total depoliticization.

First of all, the function of all these texts within the context of this publication is to expand the critique of capitalism to include a critique of all the normative practices contained in capitalism as a hegemonic power structure, primarily of the First World of capital, and then also of all the other actors involved in maintaining the hierarchies of exploitation.

Since the region of the former Yugoslavia is still undergoing the obscene process of the so-called transition to a free market economy, dictated by the colonial centre in the West and carried out by a politically impotent ethnocentric nation state, the role of this publication is to contribute to the interpretation of these processes as processes of a devastating derogation of the political role of the state, the concept of political control of society and devastation of society in general as a collective which transcends, that is, which should transcend the centrality of ethnicity. This publication, then, establishes a structural connection between the reportedly separated concepts of modernization and the establishment of capitalist hierarchies of exploitation.

In this sense, all those processes –such as the depoliticization of culture, subjecting culture and art to the logic of the free market, that is, separating the state from culture– which are presented in the public discourse by the ruling elites and free market proponents as strategies and ideological principles necessary for a transformation of society, politics and the economy into functional modern societies –are viewed in this publication as strategies and ideological principles serving to establish capitalist modernity only. This publication, then, positions itself radically against the imposition and legitimization of such an ideological supernarrative wherein only the hierarchies of exploitation, radical class and ethnic divisions and the impotence of politics reduced to an administrative professional category will be functional to the detriment of society which has yet to be politicized and/or reinvented as a collective whose needs surpass the needs of the free market and the specific actors who profit the most from its logics.

WITHIN THE IMAGE

JONATHAN BELLER

Portions of this essay were originally published as 'Wagers Within the Image: Rise of Visuality, Transformation of Labour, Aesthetic Regimes' in Culture Machine, vol. 12, 2012; http://www.culturemachine.net.

Let us examine a few consequences of the industrialization of the visual. As IPO[1] after IPO seem to demonstrate, to look is to labor: looking itself is posited as value-productive labor. We know this now. In the cinematic mode of production this generalizes to what I called 'the attention theory of value'.[2] Today, after the internet revolution (or, perhaps equally, counter-revolution), this relation between screen-time and social production is increasingly pre-supposed. Of course the energy levels, control modules and digitized metrics of interactivity have been vertiginously intensified. Here we must remark that with the digitization of the screen as socio-biological interface, with the ramification of both its functionality and the intensive development of a metrics of attention, the stock prices of media companies such as Google are what they are because they are exploits: schemas for the expropriation of value produced by the users (and therefore the used). Early dot.com markets picked up on this shift before it was widely understood. Today, this arrangement of screen-cybernetics along with an increasingly precise metrics of attention has its sights on nearly every aspect of lived and to-be-lived time, even those forms of time that are engaged in an organized struggle against capitalist forms of domination. As has been remarked, the perception of Facebook's and Twitter's future monetization potential increases with every 'Twitter revolution': unrests in Tunisia, Cairo, Madrid and New York become bankable events for new media corporations in a way at once departing from and analogous to what news has long been for print and television.

This interface between spectator and social machinery, realized as 'the image' (which received rigorous critical analysis by the Frankfurt School, the 'situationists' (Debord) and feminist film theory), has been generalized to the omnipresent screen and is also being extended to the other platforms and senses: 'the computer,' 'the tablet,' and 'the cellphone'—all of which appear to be increasingly similar. Now, of course, the program is being extended to sound, smell, touch and taste—music and game sounds, obviously, but also programmed shopping environments (which themselves extend into the urban fabric) organized by architecture, texture, scent, and arguably salt, sugar and fat. These innovations and their convergence (towards the omnipresent, omnivorous and indeed

---

1   Editor's Note: IPO stands for Initial Public Offering or the launch of a company on the stock market.

2   J. Beller, *The Cinematic Mode of Production: Attention Economy and the Society of the Spectacle*, Lebanon, NH: Dartmouth University Press, 2006.

omniscient cyber-spatialized mall-military-prison-post-industrial cosmopoplex) bring about new levels of interactivity as well as new and ever more elaborate metrics for the organization and parsing of attention-production.

Such a transformation of the role of visuality, sensuality and their media technologies in social production and reproduction necessitated the formulation of the above mentioned attention theory of value, which reduces to the labor theory of value at sub-light (sub-cinematic) speeds but allows value formations to persist for a while in the electronic matrix in non-monetized forms. The theory posits that attention produces value in at least three ways:

1. Attention valorizes media bytes and pathways in ways that can be monetized — paintings, films, war propaganda, advertisements — and monetized on spec: Yahoo, Google, Facebook, Twitter, Groupon (these are all forms of expropriation through privatization of the commons). While there are various levels and/or strategies for the valorization of attentional labor (from ticket sales, to the sale of advertising, to the IPO), what needs to be remarked upon is the still intensifying capitalist ramification of the domain of the visual and, more generally, the sensual. This domain (remember the shared institution called privacy?), formerly part of the commons, is now pitted, furrowed and trolled by the avatars of private entities bent upon the capture of formerly extra-economic activities: from accessing water, to looking around, to thought. The extent of this transformation that amalgamates attention with privately owned mediation has completely reorganized the logistics of perception, along with the mental functions that have perception as their basis (which is to say all conscious, and arguably the majority of unconscious processes, including language-function) on a planetary scale.

2. Thus we can say that the techno-economic shifts marked by cinema and its legacy technologies utilize attention to retool spectators, reworking on a minute-by-minute basis forms of social know-how, of needs, of semiotic and affective capacities, and demanding a constant revamping of 'the soul' (or of soullessness — as the case often seems to be). Workers, prosumers, playborers and those described by Flusser in a different context as 'functionaries' (those who work within the program of the camera) ready themselves and are thereby readied for the developing exigencies of the market.[3]

3. Over time visuo-attentional transformations as indexed by emerging media technologies reorganize (i.e., reprogram) language-function along with the imaginary and performativity such that the daily retoolings can be dialectically incorporated into, or functionalized by the daily advances in technical interfaces. Althusserian 'know-how', the capacity to work for capital produced in schools and other 'ideo-

---

3   J. Beller, *The Cinematic Mode of Production: Attention Economy and the Society of the Spectacle*, Lebanon, NH: Dartmouth University Press, 2006.

logical state apparatuses',[4] receives ever more penetrating and subtle elaboration through the techno-capitalist capture of the 'cognitive-linguistic'. It thus participates in what Virno, giving new life to a term from Marx, effectively identifies as the subsumption of 'the general intellect'.[5] In a recent remark, Žižek has noted that what Bill Gates accomplished with proprietary software was the privatization of part of the general intellect, which we now rent.[6] The result is that privatized media are omnipresent in the praxis of consciousness, never more than a couple of interfaces away from any and all attentional practices, such that attention to any aspect of life becomes a form of production in the social factory of capitalism.

Most of the relations discussed above could be, and indeed were, derived, in one form or another, pre-internet: they were already inherent in cinema and television, even though they have become fully manifest only in the so-called digital age. However, given that capital itself imposed a relentless digitization of life beginning in the 15th century, it is more accurate to think of today's 'digital revolution' as Digitality 2.0. These relations of communication and social cooperation were therefore incipient in the first digital revolution, that of capital itself.

Thus, early in the 20th century, one could already see that the extension of media pathways was, in fact, the further ramification of the life-world by capital-logic. The communist revolutionary filmmakers marked capital's encroachment on the visual as a site of struggle; Third Cinema (the cinema of decolonization), in Solanas' and Getino's manifesto, famously asserted that for the purposes of colonialism Hollywood was more effective than napalm (2000). Today the habitation of the senses by the logic of capitalized visuality is widespread, structuring desire, performance, perception and self-perception on a world scale, even in the most unlikely of places. For example, a recent essay by Danny Hoffman entitled 'Violent Virtuosity: Visual Labour in West Africa's Mano River War' argues that the spectacular crimes against others in the region are precisely that: spectacles of maiming and mass murder designed to garner attention in a world-media system (which includes broadcast news, the internet and the U.N.) that rewards Africa for specific kinds of self-production.[7] As Hoffman demonstrates through a close analysis of photographic and videographic materials, 'This was a war structured by the economy of attention. To profit in this economy, combatants and non-combatants were required to

---

4   L. Althusser, 'Ideology and Ideological State Apparatuses,' *Lenin and Philosophy and Other Essays,* trans. B. Brewster, Monthly Review Press, 1971.

5   P. Virno, *A Grammar of the Multitude,* Cambridge: MIT Press, 2004.

6   S. Zizek, 'The Revolt of the Salaried Bourgeoisie', *London Review of Books,* Vol. 34 No. 2, (26 January, 2012): 9-10.

7   D. Hoffman, 'Violent Virtuosity: Visual Labor in West Africa's Mano River War,' *Anthropological Quarterly,* Vol. 84, no. 4 (Fall, 2011): 949-976.

play to an audience that they knew was there, but often could only sense or apprehend in the most abstract way'.[8] Although this should be obvious it bears emphasizing: just because there is no computer in the room does not mean that one escapes its program.

One sees two significant factors in this global distribution of the logistics of the image interface: first, that the struggle for attention is a struggle for existence at many levels, and second, that restricting ourselves to categories that are marked only as politico-economic ones does not allow us to resolve the specific aspects of this struggle. Very simply, race, gender, nationality and other 'socio-historical' categories must therefore be thought of in their economic determinations within (and in excess of) the attention economy.

Within the Image / The System of Global Apartheid

The increasing power of visual and digital media gave rise to new forms of cultural imperialism (which, in case there was ever any doubt, is actually real imperialism by other or additional means). Martin Jay has identified various 'scopic regimes of modernity,' Regis Debray analyzes the emergence of what he calls the 'videosphere' which overtakes the 'logosphere' in the 19th century and Nick Mirzoeff in *The Right to Look* identifies complexes of visuality spanning the plantation (1660-1865), imperialism (1857-1947), and military industrialism (1945-present, Mirzoeff's periodizations).[9] We can clearly grasp from this intensification of the visual (however periodized and parsed) that capital targets not just territory but also consciousness, visual relations and the imagination itself in its struggle to organize production—which is to say, value-productive labor, and therefore corporeal performance. Capital's geographical expansion outwards is accompanied by a corporeal corkscrewing inward. Therefore, the visual, the cultural, the imaginal and the digital—as the de/re-terriorialization of plantation and factory dressage, Protestant ethics, manners and the like—are functionalized as gradients of control over production and therefore necessarily of struggle. This struggle for shares of social wealth is at once over images and within images.

The movement from print and semiotics to visuality and affect, which could broadly be said to characterize the current politico-economic transition from the paradigm of the factory to that of the social factory, dialectically produces the increasing slippage of the signifier from the signified. This slippage and the consequent vanishing of the Real should be historicized and thus understood as a result of the penetration of the life-world by images; the increasing gap between signifier and signified indexes technical degrees of social cyberneticization and real subsumption. In historical order, linguistics, psycho-

---

8   Hoffman, 'Violent Virtuosity', p. 952

9   First source: M. Jay, 'Scopic Regimes of Modernity,' In *Vision and Visuality*, New York: The New Press, 1988. Second source: Debray, R. *Media Manifestos*. London: Verso, 1996.

analysis, semiotics, deconstruction, postmodernism, virtual reality and reality-TV are all symptoms and accommodations of the scrambling of traditional language function by the intensification and increasing omnipresence of images. As argued in *The Cinematic Mode of Production*, the rise of late-19th and 20th century humanistic disciplines can be characterized by innovations in their treatment of language and therefore can be used to index or periodize the quantitative intensification of visuality.[10] Each intensification of the disruption of linguistic function by images along with the consequent denaturing of 'natural' language requires a new discipline capable of negotiating a receding Real; the sheer quantity of visual processing required by techno-capitalism inaugurates changes in the qualities of thought. The linguistic commons along with its ability to slow down images and configure the Real is put under siege by visual and then digital culture. This siege results in a continuous and radical re-programming of the cognitive-linguistic. The structure, functions and capacities of words themselves today bear the mark of digitiza- tion. Though this hypothesis remains to be demonstrated in detail, we might glean from the mutations in the form of literature during modernity and post-modernity the breadth and consequences of such transformations. A line drawn from the fragmentation of nar- rative at the turn of the 20th century to the veritable demise of English departments at the turn of the 21st pretty much tells the recent story of language's purchase on the world. If we were serious about taking the measure of linguistic decay, the withering of the Real, the absolute failure of semiotics and, more generally, of representation we could ruefully add to the evidence the 2012 U.S. Republican primary debates.

If capital expands through the development of visuality and the consequences of visual- ity include the evisceration, or at the very least, the reprogramming of linguistic capac- ity, then it is clear that socio-historical categories, themselves nothing other than the organization and semioticization of appearances, are also economic ones. While there is significant work tracking the interpenetration of economic vectors and those of race, nation and gender, disappointingly, it has also been possible for a self-identified leftist political economy to view racial and gendered formations as somehow epiphenomenal. This is a political as well as an analytical error. 'Race' and 'gender' are from (at least) the early modern period onward ineluctably tied to scopic regimes and therefore to eco- nomic ones. In other words, these dynamics are constitutive of technologies themselves. Thus it is incorrect to just state, for example, that photography objectifies women or racial minorities. Rather, one has to see the social role of the media platform as also constitutive of the platform. What photography 'is' has everything to do with its social functions, meaning that the objectification of women is part of what photography is, and the legacies of colonialism and slavery are embedded in its history and technical form.[11]

---

10   J. Beller, *The Cinematic Mode of Production: Attention Economy and the Society of the Spectacle*, Lebanon, NH: Dartmouth University Press, 2006.

11   J. Beller, 'Camera Obscura After All: The Racist Writing With Light,' In Jonathan Beller (ed.) *The Scholar and Feminist Online, Special Issue: Feminist Media Theory, Iterations of Social Difference*, 2012.

Otherwise, one grasps a platform fetishistically, as a reification of social relations. IBM developed the punch card to cross-reference German populations for Nazis looking for Jews, gypsies and homosexuals during the Holocaust and this development was a precursor to modern computing.[12] The social function is embedded in the machine, just as the role of computation in financialization and in the organizing of labor practices in China is also part of the meaning of the computer. Race and gender are endemic to technological form and technological form is endemic to political economy. To argue otherwise is to engage in technological determinism and fetishistic abstraction.

The investor consolidation of major industrial media platforms, from photography through cinema, video, reality-TV (which, for a decade at least, has made the hyphen between 'reality' and 'TV' mandatory) and the ambient computer is to be understood in part as a series of endeavors to profitably manage the transformed and transforming situation of language, race and gender vis-à-vis real transformations in techno-social mediations. Here we might identify four fundamental visual media shifts along with their disciplinary consequences: the visual marking and promulgation of race and gender differences alongside modern sociology (Stage 1: the art of photography); Hollywood's splicings of black musical talent onto white faces and the generalization of montage alongside psychoanalytic attention to language's break-down products and the dream as rebus (Stage 2: the rise of cinema); the promulgation of a mythically all-white, con-sumerist world bent on denying racism and imperialism on U.S. television alongside deconstruction's placing of the signified, experience, the Real and 'being' under erasure (Stage 3: television/video); the emergence of virtuality alongside the imperative to virtu-osity (Stage 4: digitality). Taken together these periodized clusters assemble techniques of subjectivity, of profitably re-mounting a worker-subject able to function in a political economy characterized by the long movement of value extraction from the scene of the plantation and factory floor to that of the deterritorialized factory, aka the scene of the screen and the social factory. Together these stages create the conditions of possibility for the current regime of Global Apartheid.

Clarity about the reconfiguration of subjectivity, language function and of interiority by the intensification of visuality, along with the consequent recession (devaluation) of the signified (Real) vis-à-vis the inflation of the sign (image) reveals that there is not a single iteration of social form that is separable from political-economic history. This dialectic further insists that we consider the mediological basis, that is, the system of support-apparatus-procedure that Regis Debray argues underpins 'mediological' transmissions (in his view incorrectly identified for the better part of a century as 'communication'), of some other recent endeav-ors to treat the transformation of the value form and the transformed situation of labor.[13]

---

12   E. Black, *IBM and the Holocaust: The Strategic Alliance Between Nazi Germany and America's Most Powerful Corporation*, Washington, D.C.: Dialog Press, 2012.

13   R. Debray, *Media Manifestos*.

In *Empire,* for example, Hardt and Negri return to Marx's idea of social cooperation as endemic to production and argue for the real subsumption of society by capital. This real subsumption is stated as a fact, but we might ask how is it accomplished? What is the material basis of subsumption? What are the media of Empire? Paolo Virno (2004) has argued convincingly that capital has captured the cognitive-linguistic capacities of the species. Pointedly, he argues that we are now all virtuosos who perform speech acts in accord with 'the score' orchestrated by capital—this, precisely, is the operation of the general intellect. Post-Fordist production requires virtuosity for the maintenance of capital expansion. Our cognitive-linguistic abilities have been conscripted and expropriated. But again, what are the mediological conditions of possibility of post-Fordism, and what are the raced and gendered dimensions of the 'servility' that Virno identifies?

Relatedly, we also have the work of Maurizio Lazzarato (1996), Christian Marazzi (2010),Tiziana Terranova (2003) on 'free labor' and 'cognitive capitalism,' providing us with a set of post-Fordist variants in which, given the sublime expansion of the financial system, virtuosos, by and large, accommodate themselves and their situations to the requisites of capitalist society in the performance of cognitive labor in a way which, according to some of these theorists, renders value immeasurable and the significance of post-Fordist input potentially undecidable.

One might identify in these innovative modes of conceptualization a relatively unacknowledged debt to the apparatus theory of Louis Althusser (1971), to feminism (Kristeva 1982, Cixous, 1994, Haraway 1991) and Marxist feminism (Fortunati, 2007; Maria Mies, 1999), to de/post-colonial and critical race theory (Fanon, 2008; Spillers, 1987; Spivak, 1999), and to media theory. However, the dominant post-Marxist arguments could be more cognisant of their conditions of possibility, both in terms of the history of raced and gendered labor (the socio-political *tekhnè*) that inaugurated the very changes in the mode of production being theorized, and in terms of the intellectual debts owed for their own theoretical formulations. This debt is a matter of citational politics, clearly, but not in any simple sense. These theories have been built upon the labor of long suffering communities as well as on their labor of insurrection and insurrectionary critique. For, let us agree to consider it a fact that revolutionary energies large and small have advanced planetary intersubjectivity in their quest for liberation even if these same energies have been domesticated by the financialization of media platforms. We must therefore be relentlessly critical when we observe that in spite of the mass basis of mediological transformations, some critical micro-cultures now proceed as if the only people worth having a conversation with are those avid readers of Badiou and Agamben, a posture that belies the highly circumscribed standpoint of the Franco-Italian insights. This insularity, palpable to readers with roots and affinities in queer, of color, and global south communities, underscores a widespread if disavowed complicity with racism, sexism and eurocentrism in still all too Western theory.

The dearth of awareness of these multiple debts and of the historicity of practices that form the new economic order of Empire is least true for Tiziana Terranova, who draws on feminism, cyber-feminism and critical race theory. Because of this she is sometimes wrongly perceived as being less original and innovative than her male counterparts. However, in arguing that 'the digital economy [i]s a specific mechanism of internal "capture" of larger pools of social and cultural knowledge [and that t]he digital economy is an important area of experimentation with value and free cultural/affective labor', Terranova is clear that the exploit of digital capitalism draws upon practices and inequalities that were 'always and already capitalism'.[14] In other words, for her at least, racism and sexism are embroiled in capitalism, and it would seem senseless to talk about (or critique) the latter in the absence of the former.

Given these observations, one should see that the concrete elements of the social: the ideological state apparatus, racial formations, the visual turn, the cultural turn, the feminization of labor and the servility and virtuosity of cognitive capitalism as part of the same equation. This is one in which the capitalized image reconfigures cultural praxis as a wholesale production site in ways that impose servility and would delimit and even foreclose the emergence of practicable anti-capitalist, anti-patriarchal, anti-racist and anti-imperialist speech-acts. Material formations precisely delimit speech-acts thus, because, generally speaking, the post-Fordist attention economy still depends upon the patriarchal, white-supremacist, imperialist organization of the global imaginary to maximize returns. The ambient machines of the social, be they concrete machines (cameras, cell phones, networks) or abstract machines (races, laws, nations) are in fact real abstractions, that is, cut-n-mixable instruments available for the virtuosic configuration of social relations such that they adhere to the requisites of raced and gendered capitalist exploitation.

To give but one example here of how a critique cognisant of these relations might take form, Cindy Gao (2012) examines a series of videos by Asian-American YouTube celebrities, including vlogs of NigaHiga and KevJumba, and Wong Fu's Yellow Fever, and characterizes their practice of performing race as 'virtuosic virtuality'.[15] Without essentializing identity (Gao sees the term Asian-American as itself a form of virtuality), the construct 'virtuosic virtuality' cranks up the stakes of the virtual and suggests that, here at least, these technologically enabled performances of ethnicity are subsumed by a capitalism that still requires and indeed develops the racial regimes that are the legacy of white supremacist capitalist patriarchy. Indeed Gao shows that one can investigate this subsumption without insisting that Marxism trumps critical race theory. It is rather that in making the critique of a narrowly empowering Asian-American performativity

---

14   T. Terranova, 'Free Labor: Producing Culture for the Digital Economy', 2003, http://www. electronicbookreview.com/thread/technocapitalism/voluntary.

15   C. Gao, 'Virtuosic Virtuality of Asian American Youtube Stars,' In Jonathan Beller (ed.) *The Scholar and Feminist Online, Special Issue: Feminist Media Theory, Iterations of Social Difference*, 2012.

(narrow because achieved through the trafficking in gendered and racist stereotypes), anti-racist and anti-capitalist critique go together. To be a bit reductive, it is arguable that in the absence of anti-racist, anti-capitalist critique the cultural movement is inevitably towards a system of structural inequality that invents and indeed requires new forms of racism—which is precisely what is going on with many of the popular Asian-American YouTube celebrities (there are certain advances but somebody has to pay, e.g., women, South Asians); or, the movement is towards a critique of capitalism that sees racism as epiphenomenal rather than constitutive and therefore uncritically replicates the racist and Eurocentric assumptions of the era.

Thus equipped we must confront the fact that increasingly, every ad we see, every page we browse, every email we send, every word we say, every thought we think and every dream we have is part of the production and reproduction of capitalist society—sensu-ous labor 2.0. The various media platforms, social categories, and imaginal iterations are one with capital and these *would* script our participation in order to allow capital to think in us and through us. I italicize 'would' here because this point is both com-plex and contentious and appears to be moving towards a genuine crisis. The dialectic requires that we have it both ways. On the one hand, capitalist expropriation has never lain so closely upon thought, utterance, the imagination and bodily practices—it has engineered a networked cybernetic matrix of control, an occupation that has seized the bio-social commons. Anti-racist, anti-capitalist critique is ever more difficult to launch effectively, since the general intellect, increasingly expropriated, thinks for capital. On the other hand, and without doubt, real subsumption can never be complete if it is to matter at all, which it does, if the thoughts (and indeed the material connections to life) for example in this essay are to be anything more than a means by which you advance your career. And whilst non-proprietary file sharing, p2p, creative commons, copy-left, etc., are laudable endeavors, and 'gateways'[16] that may open to a post-capitalist society, it seems premature to claim for any of these innovations that the medium is the message. For these practices at present do not contain within themselves a genuinely revolution-ary critique or message (anti-racist, anti-imperialist, prison abolitionist, environmentalist, feminist, queer). It is not even clear that some of them are anti-capitalist.

With our language de-fanged, our critical theory suspect, and our machines and imagi-nations complicit, where to turn? I suggest below that there are discursive and aesthetic dimensions to contemporary life that are incompletely explored. Here we must reconsider the third world, its legacies of survival and heritable corporeal commons and the possible non-capitalist transmission of these resources. The reconstitution of consciousness in post-Fordism materially links each to all in ever more intensive ways and raises question of solidarity, democracy and social justice in new domains. As I will show, the attention

---

16   S. Cubitt, 'The Political Economy of Cosmopolis' in T. Scholz. (ed.) *Digital Labor*, New York and London: Routledge, 2012.

economy induces a movement from the wage to the wager, and with this shift demands an analysis of the politics of the utterance and aesthetics of survival.

Experience teaches me that when discussing the logistics of the image and social pro-duction/reproduction through digital interactivity and human attention, I am obliged to add that none of these statements regarding the violence of media-capitalism and its subsuming of the life-world as well as many of its 'alternatives', means to say that 'prior' forms of exploitation that are characteristic of feudal serfdom, slavery, proletarianization, prostitution, domestic work, migrant labor, or the labor of survival in either camps or the postmodern slum have ceased to exist. Rather these persisting modes should be viewed as conditions of dispossession which are coordinated and legitimated, marginalized or made unrepresentable by the command-control apparatus of the digital-visual via a cal-culus of the image that enlists our for-profit participation in the capitalist military-media-prison-industrial complex. From a macro-structural point of view, human becoming is bent toward two dialectically identical ends: capital accumulation and radical dispos-session. The overall result is the immeasurable violence of the worldwide suppression of democratic becoming. We participate in this totalitarian systemic practice despite the relatively clear facts that the earth is headed towards environmental catastrophe and that two billion people (the entire population of Earth in 1929) are even now laboring to survive actually existing Armageddon. Given their intimate and indeed inescapable connection to the world media-system and the attention economy, the dispossessed have thus become the living substrate of contemporary systems of representation.[17] We write our revolutionary tracts on the backs of slaves. Radical dispossession as the other side of a world-media system is in the most literal sense the condition of possibility for our contemporary thought and writing. It bears asking, under what image or images do the radically dispossessed labor? And also, what's it to you?

The questions I pose at this point concern the images written over and on the historically produced informatic black hole smothering the bottom two billion denizens of postmod-ern globality. They are questions about subalterns whom I have come to think should never be designated by the sign bare life, but, at the very least, by the sign 'bare life', now in quotation marks. The quotation marks are there so that the signifier registers its own constitutive performativity in relation to those who are being signified upon. 'Bare life' neither merely exists nor merely appears but by virtue of a signifying process—a signifying industrial complex—that codifies its messages on bodies presumed to be incapacitated and unaccommodated to such an extent that they are beyond the reach of dialogue. These bodies are thereby made to signify the limit of sociality and presumed to exist in a condition of social death. My point here is that whether it is Agamben selling philosophy books or bankers and policy-makers selling bailouts and weapons, we find

---

17   J. Beller, 'Paying Attention', *Cabinet 24* (2008), http://www.cabinetmagazine.org/issues/24/beller.php.

bodies and populations being constituted as surfaces of inscription: bodies whose living labor of survival serves to make them fodder for philosophy, statistics, political theory, entrepreneurs, militaries, banks and states. Subalterns are actively configured as the living substrate of representation for capitalist mediation. In other words, the unceasing disfiguration of the masses is the price of success, but the success belongs to someone else: the celebrity capitalists, militarized nations, and some of their aspirant followers. Such is the enclosure wrought by the world of technical images. Squatters, trash-pickers, illegals, displaced populations, post-modern slaves, and billions for whom we here have no names and whose deaths will not appear in any newspaper, attend to the histori-cally imposed exigencies of life. Their attention to the world-machine of survival, their endeavors to constitute themselves in myriad ways, underpin the spectacular-digital of meaning, agency, and global citizenship. For the world-media system, subaltern survival or death is mere raw material for semiotics, affect and intensity. As threat, tragedy, irra-tional irruption or non-entity, entire populations are bundled and sold, converted into semiotic and affective chits for capital's master-gamers.

We must register the violence endemic to the conversion of historically dispossessed others into images and signs—in addition to objects (a concern central to the work of the young urban photo-graffiti artist JR)—because in being figured as bare life, multitudes, refugees, tribes, slum-dwellers, or terrorists, and even when not being figured at all, the capitalized universe of images and signs constitutes and de-constitutes these beings (this flesh, to borrow from Hortense Spillers, 1987) for its own purposes. As entity, non-entity, iPad, auto-part, rare earth metal, securitized population or void, the now doubly dispossessed are materially and symbolically disappeared for politico-economic ends. In other words, not only global commodity-chain production (which relies on disappeared labor 1.0) but planetary semiosis and affect-formation (which relies on disappeared labor 2.0) are rooted in the biomass of a planet of persons excluded not just from meaningful dialogue, but from dialogue. It should be underscored that the movement from 1.0 to 2.0 is a movement that took place over a matter of centuries of racialization and gendered violence but is today 'noticeable' which is to say 'theorizeable' because the chickens are coming home to roost. As Aimé Césaire remarked, what was unforgiveable about the Holocaust, was not the brutality, torture and murder, what was unforgiveable was that the techniques of colonization were applied to white people.[18] People of the Global South were the first 'content providers'. Now the situation is generalized.

Understood in this way, it would appear that the result of not just history, but also of the history of representation—representation now 'fully' captured by capital, and shunted into an informatics matrix in which capital structures images and images structure sign function, and sign function is endemic to social production and reproduction—has been

---

18   A. Césaire, *Discourse on Colonialism*, trans. J. Pinkham, New York and London: Monthly Review Press, 1972.

to make democracy structurally impossible. Such is the 'reality' for which the recession of the Real stands as symptom. The material foreclosure of the logic endemic to the conceit of human being is the technical achievement that provides the historical explanation for 'being' being placed under erasure in the realm of the sign. Understanding philosophically, as it were, that with the expiration of Western metaphysics one also confronts the expiration of humanism and the conceits pertaining to 'the human' follows logically; however understanding mediologically that this emptying out of tradition called poststructuralism is consequent upon the historico-material conversion and therefore demotion of 'natural language' into one medium among media requires a materialist approach to the totality of informatic networks that avowedly post-dialectical and post-historical thought cannot easily accommodate. Admittedly, it might take a book-length study to properly historicize Jacques Derrida's *Of Grammatology* and to methodologically 'comprehend' the moment in intellectual history known as 'deconstruction' as a specific symptom of and in the long historical process of uprooting and eviscerating language. Nonetheless, one might speculate that the 'being' under erasure there was formerly assumed to be part of the commons. As Kwame Anthony Appiah question indicated in 'Is the Post- in Postmodernism the Post- in Postcolonial?' there is an intimate connection between the erosion of the birthrights of colonized peoples and the erosion of the Western birthright purportedly guaranteed by Western metaphysics. For our purposes here we may grasp that in both the material and philosophical domains the basis and the rationale for democracy have been steadily eroded. This somewhat controversial hypothesis affirms what has been discernible at least since the onset of post-modernity: because of shifts in the matrix of representation and its material underpinnings, under advanced capitalism neither reality nor being can be adequately mounted and sustained and thus neither democratic representation nor perhaps democracy is possible. From a technical perspective this is an advance. Dialectically speaking, from this historically achieved and instrumental condition of generalized simulation there is no return.

Put another way, having reached historically the general fulfillment of what Marx saw clearly as the specific experience of the wage-laborer, namely 'the loss of reality,' the real is gone and thus the aestheticization of politics is complete. It would seem that Communism must respond by politicizing simulation, which is to say, the universe of appearances mediated by abstraction, which is to say, in short, everything, however we must leave the very question of 'the political' along with the transformed ontology of 'politics' itself for another time.

References

Althusser, L. 'Ideology and Ideological State Apparatuses,' *Lenin and Philosophy and Other Essays*, trans. B. Brewster, Monthly Review Press, 1971.

Beller, J. *The Cinematic Mode of Production: Attention Economy and the Society of the Spectacle*, Lebanon, NH: Dartmouth University Press, 2006.

Beller, J. 'Paying Attention', *Cabinet* 24, 2008, http://www.cabinetmagazine.org/issues/24/beller.php .

Beller, J. 'Camera Obscura After All: The Racist Writing With Light', in Jonathan Beller (ed.) *The Scholar and Feminist Online, Special Issue: Feminist Media Theory, Iterations of Social Difference*, 2012.

Black, E. *IBM and the Holocaust: The Strategic Alliance Between Nazi Germany and America's Most Powerful Corporation*, Washington, D.C.: Dialog Press, 2012.

Césaire, A. *Discourse on Colonialism*, trans. J. Pinkham, New York and London: Monthly Review Press, 1972.

Cixous, H. *The Helene Cixous Reader*, New York and London: Routledge, 1994.

Cubitt, S. 'The Political Economy of Cosmopolis' in T. Scholz (ed.) *Digital Labor*, New York and London: Routledge, 2012.

Debray, R. *Media Manifestos*, London: Verso, 1996.

Fanon, F. *Black Skin, White Masks*, New York: Grove Press, 2008.

Fortunati, L. 'Immaterial Labor and Its Mechanisation' in *ephemera* 7(1, 2007): 139-157.

Flusser, V. *Towards a Philosophy of Photography*, trans. A. Matthews, London: Reaktion Books, 2000.

Gao, C. 'Virtuosic Virtuality of Asian American Youtube Stars,' in Jonathan Beller (ed.) *The Scholar and Feminist Online, Special Issue: Feminist Media Theory, Iterations of Social Difference*, 2012.

Haraway, D. 'A Cyborg Manifesto,' in *Simians, Cyborgs and Women*. New York and London: Routledge, 1991.

Hoffman, D. 'Violent Virtuosity: Visual Labor in West Africa's Mano River War,' *Anthropological Quarterly*, Vol. 84, no. 4 (Fall, 2011): 949-976.

Jay, M. 'Scopic Regimes of Modernity', in *Vision and Visuality*, New York: The New Press, 1988.

Kristeva, J. *Powers of Horror: An Essay on Abjection*, New York: Columbia University Press, 1982.

Lazzarato, M. 'Immaterial Labour' in M. Hardt. & P. Virno (eds), *Radical Thought in Italy: A Potential Politics*, Minneapolis: University of Minnesota Press, 1996, pp. 133-147.

Marazzi, C. *The Violence of Financial Capitalism*, New York: Semiotext(e), 2010.

Mies, M. *Patriarchy and Accumulation on a World Scale*, London: Zed Books, 1999.

Spillers, H. 'Mama's Baby, Papa's Maybe: An American Grammar Book,' *diacritics* 17: 2 (Summer, 1987): 65-81.

Spivak, G. *A Critique of Postcolonial Reason*, Cambridge: Harvard University Press, 1999.

Terranova, T. 'Free Labor: Producing Culture for the Digital Economy', 2003, http://www.electronicbookreview.com/thread/technocapitalism/voluntary.

Virno, P. *A Grammar of the Multitude*, Cambridge: MIT Press, 2004.

Zizek, S. 'The Revolt of the Salaried Bourgeoisie', *London Review of Books*, Vol. 34 No. 2, (26 January, 2012): 9-10.

NEUTRALIZING ENGAGED SUBJECTS IN THE CREATIVE CITY

JOSEPHINE BERRY SLATER

This article is a version of a lecture given by the author in the course 'Biopolitics and Aesthetics', Centre for Cultural Studies at Goldsmiths University.

During the Blair government, a new criminal offence was passed for nearly every day spent in office—this period saw the biggest expansion in the legal regulation of conduct of any time since the end of WW2. This was also a period which saw an explosion in the commissioning of public art across Britain—a commissioning frenzy, buoyed by the liquidity of the financial bubble, which has consequently been called 'the public art bubble'. I think these phenomena can be linked, because what they represent are two prongs of a pincer that form a governmentality that acts to engage and activate subjects with the one prong, while neutralizing them with the other. Or put another way, it acts to engage certain capacities, conducts and valorizable behaviors—not least the participation in aesthetic spectatorship—while at the same time disabling, discouraging and disallowing other forms of conduct deemed disruptive to the smooth functioning of the state and some of its principle activities; namely the production of a large enough, healthy, peaceable, active and economically productive population. These two phenomena—the offense bubble and the public art bubble—can also be linked as governmental strategies for managing the antagonisms and painful inequalities of neoliberal capitalism as it comes to bear upon the everyday spaces of life in post-industrial urban society.

We are looking at a complicated conjunction of issues—neoliberal urban development, the legal regulation of behavior, and the role of public art within the post-industrial city—each has its own specificities, developmental history and extensive body of knowledge attached. But what I want to do here is to thread them together according to certain 'regulatory ideas', as Michel Foucault would say, which intersect and bind together aesthetic, governmental and economic fields. The first ones I want to think about are the concepts of 'event' and 'milieu'. The act-painting of the '40s and '50s, and the Happenings of the '60s swept the artwork clean first of representation, and then more broadly of 'retinality' as art departed pictorial and sculptural frameworks, in a bid to convene a space in which something, an 'act' and later an 'event', could occur. These twinned notions of 'act' and 'event' are deeply implicated in the multiple breaching of the art/life divide undertaken by neo-avant-garde artists of this period, and presuppose art's ability to reach out of itself to effect some kind of wider transformation of life and the world around it, whether that be: the life of the artist or the viewer as it coincides with a set of materials, ideas or conditions during the act of creation; the way parts of the sensorium and cognitive apparatus become newly open and differently sensitized through an encounter with art—what Rancière calls the 'redistribution of the sensible'—; or art's wider, subtle and unknowable infection of the social and physical environment, 'indirectly, as a stored code', as Kaprow put it.

Essential to the myriad possible manifestations of the 'event' is the notion that it takes place in an 'expanded field' that entails a potentially infinite series of elements; a field that admits new contextual, environmental, social, sensual, emotional, institutional, political and material dimensions into the conception of the artwork. This expansion could be understood as a growing reflection on and recursive folding inwards of the artwork's relationality. This folding inwards of the world, and unfurling outwards of the artwork, leads in numerous directions, from minimalism, to conceptualism to institutional critique, from body art, to performance to media art and net art, and so on. However, we need to maintain our focus on the notion of 'event' as a specific aspect of the artwork's expanded field of signification in order to induce an understanding of how developments in art are reflective of those of biopolitical governmentality and, for our purposes here, within the neoliberal moment of urban development. We also need to think about how the extension and flexibilization of the artwork makes itself newly available to deployment within a governmental and economic expansion that operates upon ever finer fissures of subjectivity.

In his lecture series *Security, Territory, Population* (1977-78), Foucault discusses—in the context of the development of the modern state and its governmental rationality—the mid-17th century production of a new spatial relationship of sovereignty to its territory, one in which the capital city comes to the fore. He concentrates on a text called *La Métropolitée*, written by a French protestant *émigré* called Alexandre Le Maître, for the protestant kind of Sweden. In it Le Maître puts forwards general recommendations for the good spatial layout of a territory; one which will open up the territory to the 'general network of the sovereign's orders and controls'. Without getting too distracted by the detail of his schema, what Foucault seizes on is how he draws together the problems of sovereignty with a set of specifically urban problematics. He writes,

> In short, the interesting thing is Le Maître dreams of connecting the political effec-
> tiveness of sovereignty to a spatial distribution. A good sovereign, be it a collective
> or individual sovereign, is someone well placed within a territory, and a territory
> that is well policed in terms of its obedience to the sovereign is a territory that has
> a good spatial layout.[1]

For Le Maître, the capital city is the ultimate arena for the production of an ideal set of spatial conditions of sovereignty, and the exemplary life it will induce and that will act as a model for the entire territory. Foucault then tracks the changing relationship between the development of towns and cities in the context of the production of a new *'raison d'État'*, or state reason, which began to see the population as the state's defining strength and, in response, developed a whole series of techniques to safeguard, nurture

---

1   Michel Foucault, *Security, Territory, Population: Lectures at the Collège de France 1977-1978*, New
     York: Picador / Palgrave Macmillan: 2007, p. 14.

and monitor populations. Towns and cities, naturally, became a focal point for these developing techniques as a new rationality of the state met the demands for growth, increased production and circulation imposed by a burgeoning capitalism. And here, with this new 'securitized', expanded and speculative approach to city planning, is where we connect back to the notion of the event.

Looking at the development of French cities such as Nantes and Vigny in the 18th century, Foucault identifies not only a response to the requirement to open up cities in order to better connect them to external routes, to deal with overcrowding and to eliminate dangerous elements and so-called miasmas, but also a new consideration of possible future events that are not precisely knowable or controllable. The calculation with and management of an indefinite series of accumulating and mobile units—'circulation, x number of carts, x number of passers-by, x number of thieves, x number of miasmas, and so on'—is, he says, the essential characteristic of the mechanism of security. As opposed to the 'disciplinary' structuring of space (here he means, the hierarchical spatial orderings of the Middle Ages) the securitized structuring of space 'will try to plan a milieu in terms of events or series of events or possible elements, [...] that will have to be regulated within a multivalent and transformable network'.[2] He ventures a further definition: 'The space in which a series of uncertain elements unfold is, I think, roughly what one can call the milieu'.[3] Borrowing the concept of 'milieu' from biology, and imposing it retrospectively onto the problem of city planning in this era of 17th century *Raison d'État,* Foucault continues,

> The milieu is a certain number of combined overall effects bearing on all who live in it. It is an element in which a circular link is produced between effects and causes[...] More disease will obviously mean more deaths. More deaths will mean more cadavers and consequently more miasmas, and so on. [...] Finally, the milieu appears as a field of intervention in which, instead of affecting individuals as a set of legal subjects capable of voluntary actions [...] or as a multiplicity of organisms, of bodies capable of performances—one tries to affect, precisely, a population. I mean a multiplicity of individuals who are and fundamentally and essentially only exist biologically bound to the materiality within which they live. [...] What one tries to reach through this milieu, is precisely the conjunction of a series of events produced by these individuals, population, and groups and quasi natural events which occur around them.[4]

In this lecture series, Foucault goes on to argue and demonstrate how this urban model of sovereignty, one that he says is extended paradigmatically to the whole territory

---

2 Foucault, *Security, Territory, Population,* p. 20.

3 Foucault, *Security, Territory, Population,* p. 20.

4 Foucault, *Security, Territory, Population,* p. 21.

in the form of the police state, will give way to a more agriculturally focused model of governmentality in the 18th century. His argument here is subtle: the mode of state rationality developed in the 17th century, that he identifies as *raison d'État*, entails a logic that concedes that the state is its own manifest destiny—it no longer imagines itself as becoming an empire, or ultimately as merging with the cosmic unity and temporality of the heavens. It is held in a balance of power, after the Treaty of Westphalia in 1648, with the other European states, and now turns inwards, discovering the utility of its own population which it starts to police in the interests of population expansion (which promised the freedom to pay lower wages), increased activity, greater levels of commodity production, higher levels of export and hence growing revenues to the treasury coffers.

This logic changes, however, to some degree in the 18th century, with the advent of the physiocrats and the *économistes*. While *raison d'État* is retained in so far as the state still regards itself, its continuation, as its aim and destiny, nevertheless it is filled with a different content. This involves a refinement of its method of governmentality, from one of state intervention and control (the police state), to one of *laissez-faire*. So instead of extending the spatial model of the city to the entire territory—because it is in the city that the techniques of security and policing are developed—the idea is to 'let nature take its course'. In regards to grain production, for example, the idea was to get rid of price controls and the control of import and export. This way production would be self-regulating, responding more agilely to the market value of grain, and ultimately better avoid the grain shortages and famines that were a frequent result of state intervention. The peasants would be better off, better fed and more productive.

Without wishing to go too deeply into this historical sequence, what is important is that Foucault argues both in *Security, Territory, Population* and *The Birth of Biopolitics* that from the 18th century an 'art of government' came to replace the more disciplinary and interventionist governmental reason that preceded it, and that this later art of government would retain the population as its focus, but strive to fulfil the interests of the state (higher levels of production, greater circulation and export of goods etc.) through an *economic* reason. This economic art of government is based on the notion, formulated by Adam Smith, of the 'secret hand of the market'; a quasi-natural force that can better settle the balance of competing interests than any more rigid and partial intervention of the state.

However, what is important here, and for our thinking about the links between the aesthetic blurring of art and life and biopower, is that the economic governmental reason retains the centrality of the 'event' and the 'milieu', the speculative balancing of a set of variables, which is expanded outwards from the setting of the town and its conditions, to the whole complexion of factors, interests and conditions that it needs to balance—one that would increasingly resolve into what we call 'the economy'. Perhaps we can even go as far as to say that *the economy is 'the event' par excellence* of this governmental rationality. As Foucault states many times, this entails a population-scale thinking—one which departs from earlier, religious or pastoral models of sovereignty in which the entire flock must be sacrificed to save a single soul, and conversely, the single soul must be sacrificed for the salvation of the flock—an economy of souls in which every individual matters. With biopower, what we see is the state intervening only

> To regulate, or rather to allow the well-being, the interest of each to adjust itself in such a way that it can actually serve all. The state is envisioned as the regulator of interests and no longer as the transcendent and synthetic principle of the transformation of the happiness of each into the happiness of all.[5]

In this respect, the individual ceases to be important, and of interest; but the conditions affecting the mass of interactions between individuals, the 'multiplicity of individuals', indeed the population, becomes the site of state intervention. I want to take a bit of a leap of argumentative faith, and suggest that we can plot a related development in art from the presiding concern with the individual object—the 'hard object'—as it is sometimes called with reference to sculpture, to an increasingly distributed aesthetic field of attention and concern. It is interesting to consider this shift in terms of a movement from the depth model of the Christian and enlightenment subject, in which all orders of experience are of moral if not economic importance, to a flattened model of the secular and biopolitical subject in which the individual becomes a moment, or the centre of a contingent set of effects, within a mobile series of interactions. We must, of course, be careful to distinguish between the objectives of a governmental reason concerned primarily with the economic and its attendant, opportune conditions of life, and the motivating forces behind this diffusion of the artwork into a relational field. Or, put another way, the reorientation of the aesthetic field of attention from the single object often involves a critique of individuality which heads in a very different direction from the biopolitical reconception of individuality as a unit of interaction within a field of forces and effects; one of a variety of mobile units that comprise the 'milieu' and the 'event'.

Roland Barthes' concept of the 'death of the author' and the 'birth of the reader' can be related to the notion of 'singularity'—that which defies the opposition between universal and particular, general and individual, to grasp a sense by which all universalities are particularized, given as such, but only in so far as the particular occurs this way, but could always occur otherwise; the characteristics of the particular are both being as it is, as it has occurred, but neither are they all that could potentially occur. This balance, and refusal of the general and the particular, one that allows for all the potential unrealized forms of Being in so far as it embraces Being as such, is what Giorgio Agamben calls the 'whatever singularity'. The relinquishing of the author, or the hard object, or representation, or technique, or retinality are all maneuvers through which a space is cleared, or rather a milieu is opened, grasped and excavated within which there is potential for

---

5   Foucault, *Security, Territory, Population*, p. 346.

something, the *whatever*, to occur within—call it an 'act', an 'event' or a 'singularity'. This potential to be otherwise, or merely this *potential for potential*, is related but antithetical to Foucault's concept of governmental securization in which potential occurrences are speculated on and allowed for within a system or plan that must be able to accommodate, respond to, neutralize or make use of a spectrum of potential events. For the security state the event is *pre*cuperated into a social and economic equilibrium; in the best relational artworks, the event's effects resist being put to work—they may even resist being consciously identified or understood—and operate more as a 'stored code', an unspent power with unknowable potential future manifestations—a whatever singularity.

Returning to the problematic of the city in its neoliberal mode of development—it is important to note the transition that occurred in the 1980s from the process of 'gentrification' to the state-led stimulation of 'urban regeneration'. Gentrification is a term coined by sociologist Ruth Glass in 1964 to describe the movement of affluent individuals into lower class areas of the city. The state simulation of this apparently ad hoc activity is what has been named 'regeneration'. I want to think about how this governmental simulation, or forced stimulation of a process deemed natural, bears all the hallmarks of neoliberalism's schizophrenic need to posit the naturalness of the market's ordering of social and economic processes on the one hand, while constantly needing to intervene to produce the correct conditions within which 'nature' can take its course. Here we will consider the role that creativity and public art is given in the production of a set of conditions which not only apparently stimulate growth, but also affect the behavior of subjects, of city dwellers, rendering them compatible with the desired trajectory of growth, productivity, and active social participation. How, in other words, the public display of creativity helps valorize life within an economic and biopolitical rationality. Part of this process of valorization is also, of course, to pre-empt, drive out and mask over those subjects and behaviors that cannot be put to use. In this sense, we can think about how securitization extends to creativity—perhaps we can call this the 'securitization of creativity'.

So, as noted, initially considered an ad hoc, *natural* phenomenon, gentrification has increasingly been engineered by first local and now global networks of real estate developers and speculators in step with local governments. It should immediately be said that the outcome of gentrification is usually one of increased property prices, increased revenue to local governments from property taxes and the displacement of lower income populations. The advent of 'urban regeneration' in the early 1980s was largely a state-led response to the blighting of the inner city in the wake of the twin phenomena of deindustrialization and suburbanization.[6] In the UK, it was also part of a governmental response to a virulent wave of riots that erupted across Britain's streets in the summer of 1981, from London's Brixton, Liverpool's Toxteth, Birmingham's Handsworth, to Leeds'

---

6   For a longer development of these arguments and history see, Josephine Berry Slater and Anthony
     Iles, *No Room to Move: Radical Art and the Regenerate City*, Berlin: Mute Books, 2010

Chapeltown. During this hot summer, dispossessed populations vented their rage and contempt for a system that treated them as surplus to requirement; both neglecting and harassing them by turns. These riots—often cast as race riots—were not only a response to high unemployment (or Thatcher's planned unemployment), biting poverty and the degenerating of housing stock, but also the aggressive policing of the non-white working class population who were subjected to discriminatory and heavy-handed policing, under 'sus' law—the police power to stop and search preemptively, purely on the basis of suspicion. Poet Levi Tafari put it this way:

> Living inna Liverpool is living in hell look pon the places where we have fe dwell them have we under a political spell bad housing unemployment and the depression as well.[7]

And how did the British state respond to the uprising and discontent of significant pockets of its population? Then Secretary of the Environment, Michael Heseltine, was dispatched around the country in a helicopter, to consult with so-called community leaders. The outcome? A series of 'Garden Festivals' around the UK, which offer an early model of 'cultural' regeneration. These festivals combined the production of a series of ornamental gardens with pop-cultural hagiography—in Liverpool, for instance, the festival included a yellow submarine and a statue of John Lennon. They were typically placed in derelict industrial sites near to working class areas, and unlocked large tranches of public money to clear sites, purify land, improve transport links and eventually transfer land to private developers. At each of the Garden Festival sites, special agencies such as the Merseyside Development Corporation were established to attract private capital investment and lead regeneration in areas undergoing post-industrial decline; these QUANGOs were directly appointed by the minister and overrode local authority planning controls—a measure which would pre-empt later large-scale redevelopment projects of the 90s and 00s.

This mode of addressing social unrest and infrastructural decline exhibits several characteristics of the biopolitical governmentality we have been discussing. The decision to clear, purify and deregulate public lands constitutes a massive subsidy to the private sector which is courted and effectively underwritten to take over the state's previous role of city development. (Soon after the festivals had ended, most of the expensively treated land they occupied was sold off to developers—an outcome that made the entire cultural experiment seem like mere foreplay). This is a prime example of the schizophrenic genuflecting to and artificial stimulation of market activity which is apparently better able to regulate social and economic activity than the state. This is also what David Harvey has termed the 'entrepreneurial' mode of municipal government which no longer directly addresses the material and social needs of inhabitants through the provision of services and the planning, building and maintenance of infrastructure, but which instead presents

---

7   Levi Tafari, *Liverpool Experience*, [Germany]: Michael Schwinn, 1989.

cities and city districts as attractive commodities whose inhabitants provide 'social and cultural capital'—effectively, just another business opportunity competing against others for inward investment from portfolio capitalists. Cultural events and signature art and architecture are of course key to this branding and selling of the city—a familiar strategy which explains much of the state subsidized public art bubble of the boom years.

Another key biopolitical characteristic witnessed in the response of the Thatcher government to the misery and desperation of inner-city populations is the use of the 'state of exception' witnessed through the suspension of local planning laws within designated parts of the city. Actions such as these expose the state's ultimate externality to its own laws which must, Foucault argues, be temporarily suspended in order to attain the very ends of the state, namely its perpetuation. (We should note, however, that Agamben sees the state of exception as having become sovereignty's permanent condition of operation within capitalism).[8] Quoting Chemnitz, the 17th century political theorist, Foucault describes the relationship of the state to its own laws thus:

> In fact, *raison d'État* must command, not by 'sticking to the laws,' but, if necessary, it must command 'the laws themselves, which must adapt to the present state of the republic'. So, the *coup d'État* does not break with *raison d'État*. It is an element, an event, a way of doing things that, as something that breaches the laws [...] falls entirely within the general horizon, the general form of *raison d'État.*[9]

The *coup d'État* itself must happen almost without the population knowing, under the blanket of darkness and secrecy, presenting it with a *fait accompli*. It is interesting to consider the role of culture as part of the theatrical *mise-en-scène* that allows this micro-*coup d'État* to occur. The yellow submarine blinds us from the real, underlying economic exchanges. A further biopolitically paradigmatic aspect of the Thatcher government's response was its attempt to intervene in the conditions of life to produce effects of 'happiness' and 'well-being' as a way of maintaining control and boosting the co-operation and productive activity of its subjects. Speaking of the development of policing in the 17th century, during the emergence of *raison d'État*, Foucault writes,

> So with the police there is a circle that starts from the state as a power of rational and calculated intervention on individuals and comes back to the state as a growing set of forces, or forces to be developed, passing through the life of individuals, which will now be precious to the state simply as life.[10]

---

8   Cf. Giorgio Agamben, *Homo Sacer: Sovereign Power and Bare Life*, Palo Alto: Stanford University Press, 1998.

9   Foucault, *Security, Territory, Population*, pp. 261-262.

10   Foucault, *Security, Territory, Population*, p. 327.

He goes on to say that this circle will pass through more than just the life of individuals, but through their 'convenience', their 'amenity', something which amounts to 'more than just living'—all of which the police were charged with ensuring through their surveillance, regulation and control of the dense interactions between individuals, especially in the towns and cities. This concern for the individual's 'better than just living' he writes,

> Must in some way be drawn on and constituted into state utility: making men's happiness the state's utility, making men's happiness the very strength of the state.[11]

Although Foucault describes the police state as a 17th century phenomenon, something which recedes firstly within the ideology of *laissez-faire*, and later neoliberalism's apparent deregulatory activity, I think it is clear that the conjunction of what we could call population optimization, short-handed as the 'nanny state' and its proliferating interventions into life, and the utilitarian deployment of happiness, shorthanded as the culture industry, suggest that this correlation of police work and the manufacture of happiness hasn't disappeared but only shifted form. The roll out of an alternating sequence of either mega-sculptures (Gormley's *Angel of the North*, Wallinger's proposed *White Horse* at Ebbsfleet, and Kapoor's *ArcelorMittal Orbit* tower for the Olympic site), or relational and ephemeral urban interventions, reveals something of the uneasy marriage of agendas that conspire around public art to help deliver the effects of happiness the state so badly needs to gain the acquiescence and self-regulation of subjects within the context of large-scale urban change.

It is precisely this conjunction of happiness and control that philosopher Maria Muhle wants to emphasize through her rejection of those characterizations of biopower that cast it as an aggressive takeover of life. Instead, she argues, it is a modality that possesses a positive and not merely repressive relation to life. 'My claim', she writes, 'is that biopolitics is defined by the fact that rather than merely relating to life, it takes on the way life itself functions; that it functions like life in order to be better able to regulate it'.[12] So there are positive and pleasurable aspects to the governmental subsumption of life—its life-like activity—that relate to art's desire to be more like-life and less like the moribund objects within the museum. Indeed, the production of this 'positive' relation, often entails the deployment of art for governmental and economic ends—as has been amply demonstrated by the paradigm of the Creative City. The general aestheticization of urban spaces certainly helps mark off the disciplinary city of factory work from the securitized city of immaterial production and consumption. The pain, filth and graft of production is increasingly purged from our cities (or at least from view), and with it the

---

11   Foucault, *Security, Territory, Population*, p. 327.

12   Maria Muhle in '"Qu-est-ce Que la Biopolitique?": A Conversation on Theories of Biopolitics between Thomas Lemke and Maria Muhle, moderated by André Rottman', *Texte Zur Kunst*, 73 (March, 2009), p. 136.

workers who performed this graft. In its place comes the illusion of our general conversion to a pleasurable, weightless form of production, and the accompanying figure of what in German is called the '*Bummler*', the ambler, the Bourgeois enjoyer of the city as a playground rich in cultural and retail diversions. No longer the austere streets of factory towns, but the slick and virtualized pedestrian zones of creative quarters, in which people's happiness is catered to, life is deemed 'more than just lived', and art contributes invaluably to a cultivation and passification of public space. But it is not just the use of art for the production of happiness effects and place branding, I would argue, that creates discomfort for the more conscious practitioners, but the sharing of certain characteristics by aesthetic and governmental regimes. Beyond a shared orientation towards the event and the milieu—complex fields of interrelation between life, activity and environment which entail a speculative approach to potential effects—there are other key 'regulatory ideas' operative in both realms, namely the concepts of 'engagement' and 'openness'.

In a recent interview about making art in the context of regeneration with the artist Alberto Duman, Anthony Iles and I discussed how the 'hard object' had been relegated in public art practice over the last decade or so.[13] He drew attention to how the sculptural tradition in public art has given way to 'a situation where everything but the object is the way to do public art', the normativity of which he finds disturbing. According to art historian Miwon Kwon, in her book *One Place After Another*, this normative switchover came with the critical reception of the public art exhibition *Culture in Action*, curated by Jane Jacob, in Chicago in 1993. It is worth quoting the curator's assessment of the trajectory from the site-specific object to the community-oriented public artwork to be reminded of how this development was unequivocally linked to progressive social effects, and actively delinked from the development agendas we now see harnessing it. She writes,

> As public art shifted away from large-scale objects, to physically or conceptually site specific projects, to audience specific concerns (work made in response to those who occupy a given site), it moved from an aesthetic function, to a design function, to a social function. Rather than serving to promote the economic development of American cities, as did public art beginning in the late 1960s, it is now being viewed as a means of stabilizing community development through urban centers. In the 1990s the role of public art has shifted from that of renewing the physical environment to that of improving society, from promoting aesthetic quality to contributing to the quality of life, from enriching lives to saving lives.[14]

What is interesting here is not only how she counters socially-oriented public art to economic development, but also how governmental her language sounds when she cites

---

13   Cf. 'Interview with Alberto Duman', in Slater and Iles, *No Room to Move*, pp.58-79.

14   Jane Jacob, cited in Miwon Kwon, *One Place After Another: Site Specific Art and Locational Identity*, Cambridge, Massachussetts: MIT Press, 2004, p. 111.

the objectives of this kind of work: 'stabilizing community development' and 'improving society' and 'improving the quality of life', not to mention the extraordinary grandiosity of her claim that art can save lives. Running through this equation of art's social orientation with ameliorating social effects is the implicit idea that the art can serve to activate members of the 'community', to 'engage' them in constructive dialogues, to alter their behavior. This conception of activated spectatorship, and its coupling to the blurring of art and life, presents a crucial isomorphism between aesthetics and the self-management of the subject that biopolitical info-capitalism attempts to stage. Present here is also a kind of crass identification between notions of engaged spectatorship and a literalization of activity that attempts to draw out aesthetic contemplation into immediate behavioral and social effects. In his book *The Emancipated Spectator*, Jacques Rancière exposes what he considers the *cul-de-sac* of avant-garde notions of activating the audience, from Bertolt Brecht to Guy Debord, for the imposition, finally, of a prescriptive and 'sovereign' notion of what counts as activity onto an audience contemptuously imagined as unrelentingly passive, as victims of the spectacle. Speaking of the wish to abolish the separation of active performers from passive spectators, or between the spaces of art and everyday life, in avant-garde theater he says,

> But the redistribution of places is one thing; the requirement that theatre assign itself the goal of assembling a community which ends the separation of the spectacle is quite another. The first involves the invention of new intellectual adventures, the second a new form of allocating bodies to their rightful place, which, in the event, is their place of communion.[15]

Rejecting the self-imposed necessity of theatre to literalize the 'community' of spectators occupying the theater at any one time, Rancière argues that, to the contrary,

> In a theatre, in front of a performance, just as in a museum, school or street, there are only ever individuals plotting their own paths in the forest of things, acts and signs that confront or surround them.[16]

Art, he argues, need not and should not strive to create a collectivity of its spectators. Art that attempts this fails to recognize the capacity that has always already joined people across boundaries, namely, the 'shared power of the equality of intelligence' which 'makes them exchange their intellectual adventures, in so far as it keeps them separate from one another, equally capable of using the power everyone has to plot her own path'.[17] It is easy to see the potential overlaps between the community creating

---

15   Jacques Rancière, *The Emancipated Spectator*, London: Verso, 2011, p. 15.

16   Rancière, *The Emancipated Spectator*, p. 15.

17   Rancière, *The Emancipated Spectator*, p.17.

desires of avant-gardism which neglect the singularity of the viewer's experience and thought, and the desire of the New Labour government to create a stakeholder society, a series of communities in which a place and activity is allocated to each and every one, but which takes no soul into account.

I think Anthony Gormley's public art exemplifies the stakes of this institutional takeover of engagement and participation—we see its machinations whirring around most nakedly in his 2009 work for Trafalgar Square's fourth column titled, *One and Other*. This piece entailed the rotation of a volunteer living occupant of the plinth on an hourly basis; an occupation which was filmed and archived on its associated website. In a grotesque bureaucratic aping of avant-garde notions of the audience's co-production of the work, the volunteer needed to obtain the right to participate by applying, via a website, and having their intended action vetted in advance before being given a time slot. The performances, by and large, became a theater of civil society initiatives, exaggerated presentations of identity and narcissistic exhibitionism. This work, it seems to me, operates according to the Agambanian logic of 'inclusive exclusion', a logic that uses the very act of inclusion as a means to exclude subjects from the scene of the political or the aesthetic. The artwork becomes a microcosm of the inclusive exclusion of the democratic process itself; participants, like voters, are fairly and evenly, if impersonally and bureaucratically treated, given a voice within the narrowly constructed terms of a permissible utterance and, in so doing, denied the ability to be heard, act collectively or engage in any 'act' that might rupture the normal functioning of things. They are effectively engaged in order to be neutralized, in the interests of the self-perpetuation of the state or the state-like power of Gormley's signature branding of high-profile public space.

This stake of institutionalized engagement—its logic of inclusive exclusion—is often discussed by artists who have worked within the context of regeneration as a tactic of 'soft policing' performed on those populations who will be most dramatically affected by development. Alberto Duman has described the consultative work of public artists in regeneration or 'social conflict zones' as that of appeasement. He says, 'The artist, very often is called in with a fairly backward idea that art has the capacity to negotiate, be a meeting place, art is a space where differences are negotiated because it can transcend the specifics of the situation, of time and space'.[18] And yet, he is keen to point out, this negotiating capacity of art is wielded from one side, namely by those who are driving the process of regeneration. As with the Big Society, public engagement is solicited just at the moment when the conditions which nurture and sustain community are being dismantled, through the generalized enclosures and sell-offs of public assets, the privatization and shrinkage of public services and the 'social cleansing' of non-productive life from the inner city. Far from 'saving lives', socially-oriented artworks such as Gormley's often provide the image of what Boris Groys has called the regime of 'aesthetic equal

---

18   Alberto Duman, in Slater and Iles, *No Room to Move*.

rights' as a cover for the reduction of the working class population's rights of access to the means of subsistence.

With a sharp sense of this double-sided, or as he calls it 'two-faced', character of much participatory public art, Duman submitted a highly sarcastic proposal to the Spitalfields Sculpture Prize in 2009. The sculpture was intended to be sited in the conflict zone of a relatively new corporate plaza that had been laid over the now demolished site of one half of Spitalfields Market in East London. The prize is funded by Hammerson, the developers behind the commercial development of the area over the last 15 years. Playing a 'two-faced' game himself, Duman submitted plans for a giant, 10m high 'Cleaning in Progress' sign that would be both eye-catching, amusing and provide shelter for shoppers and amblers from the elements. Of course the sting in the tail of this apparently innocuous object was that the cleaning it makes reference to is both social and literal; it commemorates those who have been purged from the area in order to make way for the high real estate and rental values it can now command, and flags up the relegation of those working class occupants who remain to the ancillary role of cleaners and service workers; the ghosts who maintain the space but for whom it isn't intended. The giant sign acts in solidarity with these ghosts who haunt and preserve the spaces of pleasure and consumption, whilst allowing the new occupants to shelter under its protective mantle.

For Boris Groys, avant-garde art's development of a regime of 'equal aesthetic rights' hinges on the idea, linked to the blurring of art and life, that the classical avant-garde 'has struggled to achieve recognition of all signs, forms, and things as legitimate objects of artistic desire and, hence, also as legitimate objects of representation in art'.[19] He sees a parallel between the aesthetic struggle for recognition, and the political struggle for the recognition and inclusion of all minorities. Within art, however, the thought that anything can potentially be recognized as art potentially leads to an entropic game where each artwork appears to be simply an arbitrary and unnecessary extension or iteration of this field of equal rights. However, he argues, art today 'operates in the gap between the formal equality of all art forms and their factual inequality'.[20] So, while recognizing the potential legitimacy of anything as art, in reality not everything is considered as such and admitted into the museum or the canon. 'The good artwork', he continues, 'is precisely that work which affirms the formal equality of all images under the conditions of their factual inequality. This gesture is always contextual and historically specific, but it also has paradigmatic importance as a model for further repetition of the gesture.'[21] I think Duman's work strikes just such a balance, elevating the readymade plastic sign to a higher power which implies the potential elevation of any profane object, whilst mobiliz-

---

19   Boris Groys, 'Equal Aesthetic Rights', in *Art Power*, Cambridge, Massachussetts: 2008, p. 14.

20   Groys, *Art Power*, p. 16.

21   Groys, *Art Power*, p. 16.

ing this banal object to signify the factual exclusion of former inhabitants who become the 'revenants' of this apparent space of open, democratic enjoyment. Put another way, the participation of the banal object in the aesthetic regime of equal rights becomes a cipher for the factual impossibility of participation within a wider regime of participatory aesthetics.

Earlier I mentioned that 'openness' was another regulatory idea that intersects governmental, economic and aesthetic terrains. As with the regime of equal aesthetic rights, the principle of openness can also happily co-exist with and co-produce factual inequalities and closed or proprietary systems. We see this everywhere from the deployment of the open standards of the web, such as HTML and HTTP to run proprietary software or for private profit, to the double standards of free market capitalism where developing countries are compelled to open up their markets and allow inward investment while economic giants like the US are able to maintain trade barriers and subsidies for domestic production. Openness itself is a kind of conceptual medium along which, as chairman for the US Business Committee for the Arts in the 80s Winton Blount once said, business can also travel. Fighting trade regulations, taxation and overt government control was not just a civic duty, he argued, but a means of keeping 'open those avenues of freedom along which art and commerce both travel'.[22]

Roman Vasseur, Lead Artist appointed to oversee the redevelopment of Harlow New Town, has argued, this reversibility of openness can also extend to who might be considered an artist in the context of creative-led regeneration. 'One can envisage a future' he says, 'where artists, or individuals with an extensive training in the visual arts and art history will be slowly moved out of this new economy in favor of "creatives" able to privilege deliverability and consultation over other concerns'.[23] It is worth considering how the energies that drive the privileging of openness as an aesthetic, technical, economic and social form waver between the political horizon of inclusion and the degraded, flattening equivalence of the value form. This has the interesting effect of driving the Beuysian claim that 'everyone is an artist' in at least two directions at once: the death of the author also presides over the birth of the professionalized creative. What this final example reveals is the extent to which governmental and economic calculation and the social engineering of happiness can move along similar trajectories as the life-oriented activities of art. But in keeping with Groys' remarks about the good artwork, the artistic attempt to promote a life which is 'more than just lived' cannot take place under the monocultural regime of human capital, or under the logic of biopolitical happiness, if it does not draw attention to the way biopolitical capitalism mobilizes individuals to create optimum effects within its own paradigm of population optimization. The good artwork that aims to act upon life takes into account the more radical horizons of openness, event,

---

22   Cited in Chin-Tao Wu, 'Embracing the Enterprise Culture', *New Left Review* 230 (1998): 30.

23   Roman Vasseur in 'Interview with Roman Vasseur', in Slater and Iles, *No Room to Move*, p. 114.

act, milieu, engagement and participation, admitting as much to the factual absence of these realities as to the potential for their potential in a wholly unspecified future form.

References

Agamben, Giorgio. *Homo Sacer: Sovereign Power and Bare Life*, Palo Alto: Stanford University Press, 1998.

Foucault, Michel. *Security, Territory, Population: Lectures at the Collège de France 1977-1978*, New York: Picador / Palgrave Macmillan, 2007.

Groys, Boris. *Art Power*, Cambridge, Massachussetts: MIT Press, 2008.

Kwon, Miwon. *One Place After Another: Site Specific Art and Locational Identity*, Cambridge, Massachussetts: MIT Press, 2004.

Muhle, Maria. '"Qu-est-ce Que la Biopolitique"' A Conversation on Theories of Biopolitics between Thomas Lemke and Maria Muhle, moderated by André Rottman", *Texte Zur Kunst*, 73 (March 2009).

Rancière, Jacques. *The Emancipated Spectator*, London: Verso, 2011.

Slater, Josephine Berry and Anthony Iles. *No Room to Move: Radical Art and the Regenerate City*, Berlin: Mute Books, 2010.

Tafari, Levi. *Liverpool Experience*, [Germany]: Michael Schwinn, 1989.

Wu, Chin-Tao. 'Embracing the Enterprise Culture', *New Left Review* 230 (1998).

THE AGENCY OF ART IN THE UNCONSCIOUS

MARC JAMES LÉGER

How can we explain the gray zone, the minimum distance between creativity and capital-ist demand? How can we understand creative autonomy and resistance in the context of renewed expectations for art to have a direct social and political utility? What can psychoanalysis contribute to art criticism as it relates to the field of politicized visual art, now more commonly referred to as socially engaged art? What does the notion of the *avant-garde* mean for cultural production in a world of networked connectivity, partici-patory ideology and creative industry dispossession? According to Slavoj Žižek, when art production is increasingly subjected to commodification, and when commodities are increasingly aestheticized, artworks are no longer able to sustain the lack in the *big Other*, understood here as the agency of belief in art's social and cultural significance.[1] One symptom of this phenomenon is the view that art today has collapsed directly into political economy. In the words of the editors of *e-flux* journal, 'contemporary art *is* neoliberalism in its most purified form'.[2] The truth of this assertion is that artworks are particularly apt as signifiers of castration. As creativity marks ever more aspects of daily life, almost any kind of work not only can, but in a kind of frenetic hysteria, must be elevated to the place of Art.[3] While this may seem a standard postmodern argument for the breakdown of the distinction between high art and mass culture, postmodernism tends nevertheless to leave belief in the aesthetic intact, proliferating through the fields of discourse it comes into contact with. In the following, I argue against postmodern relativism, however, and wish to consider instead, to paraphrase Žižek in his thinking on Christianity, 'the perverse core' of avant-garde art production.

Art for Imbeciles

In an essay on what he calls 'enclave theory', John Roberts made the somewhat startling assertion that many of the most progressive art theories of recent years (those attributed to Nicolas Bourriaud, Gregory Sholette, Grant Kester, Stephen Wright, and even theorists like Jean-Luc Nancy, Alain Badiou, Slavoj Žižek, Bruno Bosteels, Felix Guattari, Toni Negri, and Michael Hardt) represent the 'invariant core of a communist programme' that is 'largely divorced from the past', in particular, from its Stalinist Communist party organiza-tions, and is committed rather to 'culturally aestheticized [...] autonomous forms of pro-

---

1   Slavoj Žižek, *The Fragile Absolute, or, Why Is the Christian Legacy Worth Fighting For?*, London: Verso, 2000, pp. 31-32.

2   Julieta Aranda, Brian Kuan Wood and Anton Vidokle (eds), 'Editorial', *e-flux journal* 21 (2010), http://www.e-flux.com/journal/editorial-18/.

3   See Gerald Raunig, Gene Ray and Ulf Wuggenig (eds), *Critique of Creativity: Precarity, Subjectivity and Resistance in the 'Creative Industries'*, London: MayFly Books, 2011.

ductive, intellectual and creative community'.[4] What is surprising in this claim is the idea that these are invariant forms, and not significantly different. Roberts asks us to consider what all of these theorists' perspectives on radical culture have in common rather than what distinguishes them. This gesture might not be such a bad way to understand the so-called 'crisis' of art and art criticism in a world of cultural corporatization and neoliberal engineering of creative capital. Whatever contemporary art's failings in terms of pursuing revolutionary class struggle, it represents, according to Roberts, a kind of leftist bloc against what Sholette terms enterprise culture. Perhaps one of the most acerbic depictions of the art world as a rigged system of economic and social exploitation is Bruce Barber's 2008 drawing titled *Artworld Ponzi Scheme*, which shows a pyramid comprized of payers, prayers, and players, all of them trapped within a hierarchically inegalitarian system. The intrigue in this drawing, especially as it comes after the biggest financial debacle since the 1970s, is that the currency of art is premised on false claims, or even 'toxic assets'.

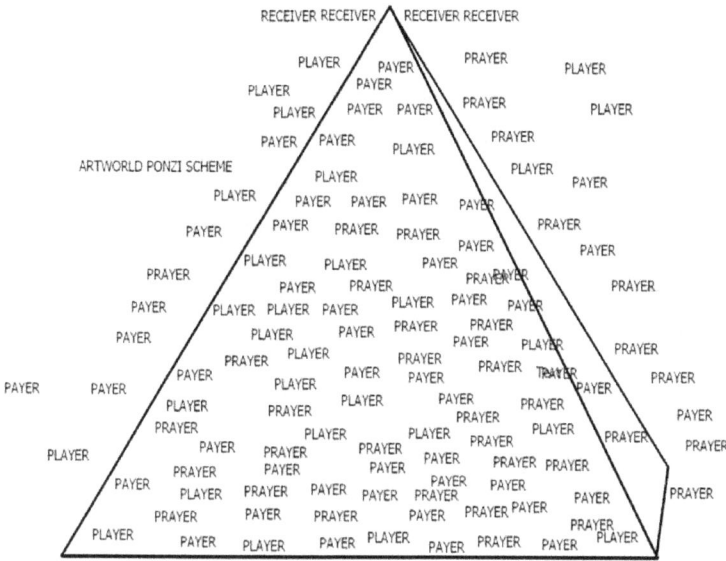

Fig. Bruce Barber, *Artworld Ponzi Scheme*, drawing, 2008. Courtesy of the artist.

The idea that art has no socially agreed upon justifications has been addressed by anthropologist David Graeber, who wonders why contemporary theorists attending an art symposium at the Tate Museum should explain the 2008 fiasco by taking recourse to avant-garde art created between 1916 and 1922.[5] His point is that we are potentially

---

4 John Roberts, 'Art, "Enclave Theory" and the Communist Imaginary', *Third Text* 23:4 (2009): 353, 358.

5 David Graeber, '"The Sadness of Post-Workerism", or "Art and Immaterial Labour" Conference: A Sort of Review', 2008, http://www.scribd.com/doc/38093582/The-Sadness-of-Post-Workerism-David-Graeber.

once again living a revolutionary moment, but that epistemological subversion through culture and post-structuralist theory seems to satisfy only liberal academics. The return to avant-gardism, he argues, effects

> a subtle form of conservatism—or, perhaps one should say conservative radical-ism, if such were possible—a nostalgia for the days when it was possible to put on a tin-foil suit, shout nonsense verse, and watch staid bourgeois audiences turn into outraged lynch mobs.

These days are gone, he argues, replaced by the immaterial labor and service economy analysis of people like Maurizio Lazzarato and Toni Negri. The art of the rich, he goes on, has more to do with the analysis of products than of social processes, floating above the mire of ordinary existence. Art today appears to contemporary political philosophers to belong to the immaterial domain, a fact that exacerbates its condition of crisis. The art world, for Graeber, is the apparatus of people who manage this crisis. Unable to define the category of art in any way that is adequate beyond its quality as something that only rich people and museums can afford to buy, the art world cannot establish its own legitimacy. Graeber then argues that the essence of politics in social life is to make people believe. Things become true if you can convince enough people to believe them. In order to play the game effectively, one must not oneself know the essence of things. He concludes from this that if the art world was to recognize itself as a form of politics, it would also need to 'recognize itself as something both magical, and a confidence game—a kind of scam'.[6] Insofar as the art world has become an appendage to financial capital, fictive capital explains fictive cultural value as well. All the players, he argues, cynics and idealists alike, draw on outmoded nineteenth-century notions of art, even those who create 'enclaves' where they can experiment with new forms of life.

Where Graeber gets at the issue is when he later argues that for all of the fictionalization that takes place across the social field, the magically created value of art is no less real. This assertion confirms the Lacanian emphasis on the reality of illusion, which contrasts to transgressions that merely try to escape the Real. In this regard, Žižek agrees with Badiou, who argues that art is a medium of truth. This also relates to the Marxist under-standing of commodity fetishism, which states that even if capitalists understand that workers produce the value of their merchandize, they nevertheless continue to believe in the miracle of exchange. The famous Žižekian example, of course, is the anecdote about Niels Bohr, who when asked if he believed in the good luck derived from a horse shoe, replied he did not, but that apparently it works even if one does not believe in it. Rather than payer, player, and prayer, then, categories that Barber leaves undefined, I would like to propose the set of three subject positions that Žižek outlines at the start

---

6   Graeber, "'The Sadness of Post-Workerism'".

of *Less Than Nothing*: the idiot, the moron, and the imbecile.[7] All three positions are premized on the Lacanian theory of the *big Other*, which stands for the heterogeneous social rules that together comprize what Lacan defines as the social symbolic. As an impersonal social agency, the *big Other* stands in for those rules that shape the unconscious of the social subject.

The first of the three is the idiot, defined by Žižek as someone who is 'too intelligent to process implicit social rules'.[8] The idiot imagines himself beyond the influence of the *big Other* and knows the rules (of art) all too well to be able to process them in a way beyond his hyper-intellectuality. As the first of two examples of idiots within contemporary art theory, both colleagues of mine, we have Sholette and his concept of 'dark matter'. According to Sholette, dark matter describes the 'shadowy social productivity' that haunts the high art world. The great many excluded practices and failed artists who keep the world of galleries, collections, and magazines going, Sholette argues, are today threatening this pyramidal system as their dark energy becomes increasingly visible. The book *Dark Matter* thus presents itself as a 'lumpenography' of this invisible mass of makeshift, amateur, informal, unofficial, autonomous, activist, non-institutional, and self-organized practices.[9] Sholette argues that art critics, art historians, arts administrators, collectors and dealers typically have little interest in creative dark matter. There is no question that the art world is made up not only of what is known about art, but involves a complex division of labor and specialized tasks that work to keep a multi-billion-dollar industry operating for the benefit of a minority of high profile artists. This system keeps the vast majority of professionally trained artists in a state of subservience and underdevelopment. The first and most general question that is asked by Sholette is what would happen if this superfluous majority went on permanent strike and gave up on the art system's means of legitimation. Contemporary high art is thoroughly connected, he says, to Art Inc. and does not hide its profit motivations. It is only those dark practices at the margins that still hold on to this former (avant-garde) task of art to challenge commercial goals. While Sholette does appreciate the labor theory of value, he suspends the understanding that most forms of culture are non-productive and rather dependent in complex ways on profits collected elsewhere in the proletarianized global marketplace. Bourdieu's sociology of art, in contrast, benefited from its use of the concept of social totality. The absence of the use of the concept of totality in Sholette's book prevents him from offering a class analysis of culture that would go beyond redistributive justice. Also, dark matter seems to share very little common ground with the avant-garde tradi-

---

7   Slavoj Žižek, *Less than Nothing: Hegel and the Shadow of Dialectical Materialism*, London: Verso, 2012, pp. 1-2.

8   Žižek, *Less than Nothing*, p. 1.

9   Gregory Sholette, *Dark Matter: Art and Politics in the Age of Enterprise Culture*, London: Pluto, 2011, p. 1.

tion of revolutionary art, whose distinct purpose is to represent the social function of art in class society. As Žižek has argued, an ideological identification exerts the greatest pressure on us when we fool ourselves into believing we are not fully identical to it. The epistemological crisis in the arts that is mentioned in Sholette's introduction to *Dark Matter* should therefore not be thought to directly reflect the crisis in global capital, though the connections between these spheres do indeed need to be drawn.

A second idiot in this set is Brian Holmes and his theory of 'liar's poker'. Holmes is one of the sharpest analysts of artistic resistance within societies of control and is also, like so many contemporary theorists, skeptical of avant-garde modes of contestation. Within the new flexible regimes of accumulation and casual freelance culture, the demands for autonomy, he argues, are diverted into new modes of control.[10] The premise of liar's poker, as he puts it, is that 'when people talk about politics in an artistic frame, they're lying'.[11] Cultural institutions, he argues, constantly demand that artists 'picture politics', playing the art game and representing those who are excluded to those who are safely nestled inside, especially transnational corporations, who then support the realm of art as a sphere that is separate from abstract financial decisions. Anti-art artists who work directly in the public sphere or on the terrain of everyday life, or within new technological and scientific landscapes, only pretend to leave behind the artistic frame. In reality they collude with curators and directors to show images of political reality. Because the latter are averse to such realism, the artist has to bluff their way through. Holmes assumes, however, that an artist involved with a social movement is an artist that has successfully challenged the guilt relations of the art system. Because of this he is deeply suspicious of the function of belief, which, he argues, is a powerful or interesting fetish, an illusion that gets players caught in the game rather than directly confronting power, as in the case of artworks that deepen the links between art activism and social movements. What distinguishes Holmes from Žižek, however, is that he does not ask us to believe even more in art and to directly assume the lack in the *big Other*—a small distinction, but a crucial one if we are to see art institutions as anything more than duplicitous. Like Sholette, Holmes is concerned that institutions seek cultural capital among 'the more radical fractions of the artistic field'.[12] The artist has to produce the ace of politics, he argues, while proving all the while that the ace is merely a joker, thereby undermining the reality of the illusion. Like so many leftists, Holmes assumes that the big Other is or can be occupied.

The second subject position outlined by Žižek is the moron, defined by 'the stupidity of

---

10   Brian Holmes, *Unleashing the Collective Phantoms: Essays in Reverse Imagineering*, Brooklyn: Autonomedia, 2008, p. 19.

11   Holmes, *Unleashing the Collective Phantoms*, p. 81.

12   Holmes, *Unleashing the Collective Phantoms*, p. 91.

those who fully identify with common sense, who fully stand for the big Other of appear-ances'.[13] Two notable cultural theorists who might in some ways fill this description are Grant Kester and Claire Bishop. Kester is a seasoned art critic with a long track record of insightful writing on the shift from public art and identity politics in the 1980s and 90s to the new phenomenon of community art in the 90s and 2000s. The type of site-specific collaborative work that he champions unfolds, he says, through an extended interaction with local communities. Like many proponents of the new tendencies, he has worked to anchor his theory of 'dialogical aesthetics' in both social and political his-tory as well as the philosophy of aesthetics. While erudite and knowledgeable, Kester's polemic, as presented in his book *The One and the Many*, is intensely prescriptive.[14] For the sake of artist groups like Park Fiction, Ala Plastica, and Dialogue, all avant-garde tactics (reduced to formalist modernism) are proscribed, including the work of leading cultural theorists like Barthes, Derrida, de Certeau, Lyotard, Kristeva, Blanchot, Badiou, Deleuze and Guattari, Agamben, Nancy, Levinas, and Rancière—anyone associated with the post-May 68 generation of postmodern pessimism and who programmatically guard against premature totalizations.

We are witnessing today a certain disenchantment with the existing parameters of avant-garde art and an attempt to rearticulate the specificity of the aesthetic in re-lationship to both the viewer and to other cultural and political practices.[15]

The leitmotif of avant-garde and theoretical post-structuralism, he argues, is the impos-sibility of social cohesion.[16] In contrast, Kester is interested in the global phenomenon and success of collaborative modes of production, as found for instance in the work of Border Arts Workshop, Group Material, REPOhistory, Gran Fury, Platform, WochenKlau-sur, and Groupo Etcetera, where emphasis is placed on multiple authorship, participatory relation to audience, and process-based activist intervention.[17] Despite his critique of what he calls the 'intellectual baroque', Kester's dialogical aesthetics retains many of the typical leitmotifs of postmodernism, especially the distinctions that are made between pluralism and an older avant-garde notion of culture that retained some links to the class politics of socialism. With globalization, I would argue, social forms have channeled culture in such a way as to give it a privileged role in economic development. According to George Yúdice, culture is today treated as an expedient, construed as a resource for

---

13 Žižek, *Less than Nothing*, p. 1.

14 Grant Kester, *The One and the Many: Contemporary Collaborative Art in a Global Context*, Durham: Duke University Press, 2011.

15 Kester, *The One and the Many*, pp. 36-37.

16 Kester, *The One and the Many*, p. 49.

17 Kester, *The One and the Many*, p. 4.

sociopolitical ameliorism and job creation, a process that coincides with capitalist ideology and biopolitical regulation.[18] The role of culture, Yúdice argues, 'has expanded in an unprecedented way into the political and economic at the same time that conventional notions of culture have been emptied out'.[19] Unlike Sholette and Holmes, Kester tends to underplay this problem of institutional mediation, leaving actually existing institutions all the more operative in the administration of socially engaged art.

Another critic we could add to the group of morons is Claire Bishop. Bishop is well-known for her 2004 *October* essay in which she criticized Bourriaud's relational aesthetics for its rhetoric of democracy and emancipation.[20] The open works advocated by contemporary critics like Bourriaud foreground interaction rather than contemplation and engagement rather than passivity and disengagement, assuming that these former modalities are inherently political and emancipatory. She argues that Bourriaud wants to equate aesthetic judgement with political judgement. 'But how', she asks, 'do we measure or compare these relationships?'.[21] Dialogue, she says, is assumed in advance to be democratic, excluding other modalities, like autonomy, antagonism, oppositionality, destabilization, and artworks that recognize the limits of 'society's ability to fully constitute itself'.[22] She defines the autonomy of the artwork in terms of the social antagonism that is mirrored in the tension between art and society. Bishop insists that we should be better able to judge art itself and not merely better politics, and therefore acknowledge the limits of what art can do. One of the problems here is the return to the function of criticism and the assumption that art, by itself, can be the object of objective assessment. In this gesture Bishop obviates the notion of antagonism that she otherwise recognizes. While she exposes what is repressed in the idea of social harmony, she ignores how art itself acts as this agent of repression. In this regard, *Artificial Hells*, her latest treatment of participatory art, mostly expands the number of examples rather than improve the initial theory.[23] She worries about the instrumentalization of participatory art, something Kester is less troubled by, but perhaps misses the point that this apprehension is misplaced insofar as it concerns itself with art *per se* and art criticism as a means of institutional legitimation (perhaps to satisfy critics like Graeber). She very correctly recognizes that the new European cultural policies enacted under *New Labour* in the U.K. are a form of

---

18   George Yúdice, *The Expediency of Culture: Uses of Culture in the Global Era*, Durham: Duke University Press, 2003.

19   Yúdice, *The Expediency of Culture*, p. 9.

20   Claire Bishop, 'Antagonism and Relational Aesthetics', *October* 110 (2004): 51-79.

21   Bishop, 'Antagonism and Relational Aesthetics': 65.

22   Bishop, 'Antagonism and Relational Aesthetics': 67.

23   Claire Bishop, *Artificial Hells: Participatory Art and the Politics of Spectatorship*, London: Verso, 2012.

social engineering but fails to produce a theory that addresses how and why art eludes such institutionalization.

I would argue, in contrast, that it is quite possible for an artwork to be valid as an autonomous and critical work and at the same time to defy institutional capture, and this, without denying the incompleteness of the social. For me to say this, I should think that I belong to the third group in Žižek's series: the imbeciles. An imbecile is someone whose mental retardation causes him to be aware of the need for a *big Other*, but who does not rely on it. The imbecile is somewhere between the idiot and the moron, who recognizes the function of language but who distrusts it.[24] The *big Other* exists, but is inconsistent. The question for aesthetics, then, is to consider in theoretical and not only sociological terms the ways in which the art world guarantees the consistency of the rules of art, allowing for dark matter to be distinguished from consecrated artists. What unites the idiot, the moron and the imbecile is the inconsistency of their belief in the *big Other* of art and, as I argue further on, this inconsistency represents the 'perverse core' of aesthetics as such.

The Reality of the Fiction

What is the significance of critical art in the context of contemporary cultural theory, within the space of culture in general, and as it is being reengineered to conform ever more tightly with the needs of accumulation—leading many to presume that avant-garde artworks and films have been made obsolete by new social relations and by the new regimes of production? Here I would like to pursue the path of the imbecile with reference to Žižek's chapter on Christianity in the opening 'Drink Before' section of *Less Than Nothing*. The trick is to not reduce theory to empiricism and to focus on the negative energy of art rather than the positivity of the social causes that artists are being increasingly expected to deal with directly. While I do not agree with those who argue that art and reparative social work or political propaganda are inherently separate activities, I do think that socially engaged art benefits from some aesthetic theorizing that goes beyond German idealism.

Žižek's attention to Hegel in *Less Than Nothing* is largely due to the overlap with Lacan and Žižek's view that among the German idealists, Hegel alone is able to sustain the idea of the lack in the *big Other* and the dialectical reversal that occurs when an epistemological obstacle is transposed directly into the Thing itself—here the work of art.[25] 'Our inability to know the thing indicates a crack in the thing itself, so that our very failure to reach the full truth is the indicator of truth.'[26] No wonder then that dark matter, to take

---

24 Žižek, *Less than Nothing*, p. 2.

25 Žižek, *Less than Nothing*, p. 17.

26 Žižek, *Less than Nothing*, p. 17.

up the metaphor, is obviated by the obsession with the celebrity star system: Picasso, Van Gogh, Ai Weiwei, Gerhard Richter, Jeff Koons, what have you. One problem in the structure of ideology, Žižek explains, is that there is no public, no symbolic agency that is there to register or witness the disasters of capitalism. What is missing is the *big Other*, the space of symbolic inscription and ideological suture. In contrast to Claire Bishop's quest to determine institutional criteria for judging participatory art, Žižek writes:

> Schoenberg still hoped that somewhere there would be at least one listener who would truly understand his atonal music. It was only his greatest pupil, Anton Webern, who accepted the fact that there is no listener, no big Other to receive the work and properly recognize its value.[27]

There are no guarantees for art and this becomes one of the principal axioms of the notion of creativity. Those who worry that all creativity is today harnessed by capital miss an important point: the form of illusory appearance remains on the surface of things and is thus closer to the Real than historical reality itself. The concern of political moralists and reformists is often to escape from the Real of illusion through some kind of transgression that seeks to show the true, so-called 'phenomenal' reality, usually by pointing to some token of reality: bodily affect, group interaction, S&P indicators, the haptic qualities of new media, etc. The idea that art criticism should be more global in scope, representing a greater diversity of experiences, is one way among many to avoid the Real of illusion.[28] What then can artworks tell us about the changing parameters of what Peter Bürger defined as the 'institution art'?[29]

The unique quality of art is that more than most other things in our social universe it can express the reality of illusion through any random object. This illusory quality is a secret, in Marx the commodity fetish, or in Lacan, the ineffable *objet a* that allows anything to be elevated to the concept of Art and allows it to be installed in the symbolic order. The artist comes closest to this understanding when he or she intervenes through the neutral position of the analyst.[30] The artist's neutrality cannot be socially localized since the art thing has no ontological reality but is a virtual point. This is what Lacan refers to in the notion of *le père ou le pire*—the oedipal father or the worse, the choice of art as the

---

27   Žižek, *Less than Nothing*, p. 29.

28   Marc James Léger, 'Art and Art History After Globalization', *Third Text* 26:5 (2012): 515-527.

29   Peter Bürger, *Theory of the Avant-Garde*, trans. Michael Shaw, Minneapolis: University of Minnesota Press, 1984.

30   Marc James Léger, 'The Subject Supposed to Over-Identify: BAVO and the Fundamental Fantasy of a Cultural Avant Garde', in Léger (ed.), *Brave New Avant Garde: Essays on Contemporary Art and Politics*, Winchester, UK: Zero Books, 2012.

worse option, which more effectively undermines the entire symbolic field. Avant-garde works represent a negative force against the organic unity of community and as such are vital to emancipatory politics.[31] Strict egalitarian emancipation cancels rather than preserves the organic unity of the hierarchical social order. Radical art operates as the obscene disavowed underside of the art world ponzi scheme. How so?

Almost every artwork preserves some aspect of the idea of art as a reserve, or background against which we can measure deviations. Art's non-art status is therefore inscribed into the idea of Art—something that Duchamp was perhaps the first artist to expound. Art is deeply atheistic, to put things in terms of belief, and perversion is at the core of the aesthetic. The obsession with the ineffable *big Other* is sublated into acts of creation, something that Lacan defines as drive. Creativity can therefore be defined as the eruption of a new form that reorganizes the social field, imposing itself as a new necessity through an act of ungrounded subjective decision, abandoned by Art and with no guarantee of aesthetic value or art world consecration.[32] The inscrutability of the aesthetic *big Other*, even as blue chip investment, is the certitude of creativity, the condition of its ecstatic production. Since art is dead and the author is dead and since therefore the function of the critic is nullified, art making and art judgments are sacrificed to a pure Otherness of subjective destitution.

Art making is a scandal that undermines art from within. Such work has a tragic self-effacing quality that socially engaged art sometimes refuses in its resentment and narcissistic hatred of the 'no' of Art. It denounces art in favor of ethics but it does so through the disavowal of the love of art. It proffers the socially networked artist as the better of the avant-garde artist but it is the latter who properly betrays the extorsion of creativity. The revolutionary artist acts unconditionally and therefore comes closest to art's expression of freedom and emancipation, insisting, much like Antigone, on symbolic demand. The creative artist is consequently excluded from the community of humans.

Holmes' notion of 'liar's poker' can be explained as the insistence on aesthetic sublimation rather than the insistence on the refusal of co-optation; it implies an awareness of the monstrosity of the game since the game is not only fixed in the symbolic order, but more radically, since through his or her act the artist believes in the game more than s/he is aware. The artist acts as though he or she is not aware of capitalist recuperation, observing the appearances, the virtuality of the illusion of the real. In the case of Barber's pyramid, the 'prayer' in the set represents a transitive function; he or she does not have to believe since belief is presupposed by the artwork as virtual entity. No wonder then that so many artists today are attempting to go beyond the making of objects, taking social interaction itself as the direct instantiation of art. This becomes possible due to

---

31   Žižek, *Less than Nothing*, p. 70.

32   Žižek, *Less than Nothing*, pp. 106-11.

the perverse core of art and is an indication of the transitivity of belief. The paradox, however, is that if we take away whatever stands in for belief, we lose the reality of the illusion and so any claim to emancipation through the community of believers is equally annulled. The function of the art world, therefore—critics, museums, magazines, even this essay—is to maintain appearances, in particular, against any agency or Master who would pretend to know everything. The master artist is the person who possesses an almost God-like ability to both make art and to simultaneously prohibit the making of art. This prohibition takes the form in capitalist society of symbolic castration through surplus value. A provisional definition of the avant-garde artist can therefore be the condition of the acceptance of the inexistence of aesthetic criteria. There are no guarantees for the social importance of artworks, only the passage from creativity to consequences. For things to happen, creation must be a condition of the truth of illusion.

References

Aranda, Julieta, Brian Kuan Wood and Anton Vidokle (eds). 'Editorial', *e-flux journal 21* (2010), http://www.e-flux.com/journal/editorial-18/.

Bishop, Claire. 'Antagonism and Relational Aesthetics', *October 110* (2004): 51-79.

Bishop, Claire. *Artificial Hells: Participatory Art and the Politics of Spectatorship*, London: Verso, 2012.

Bürger, Peter. *Theory of the Avant-Garde*, trans. Michael Shaw, Minneapolis: University of Minnesota Press, 1984.

Graeber, David. '"The Sadness of Post-Workerism", or, "Art and Immaterial Labour" Conference: A Sort of Review', 2008, http://www.scribd.com/doc/38093582/The-Sadness-of-Post-Workerism-David-Graeber.

Holmes, Brian. *Unleashing the Collective Phantoms: Essays in Reverse Imagineering*, Brooklyn: Autonomedia, 2008.

Kester, Grant. *The One and the Many: Contemporary Collaborative Art in a Global Context*, Durham: Duke University Press, 2011.

Léger, Marc James. 'Art and Art History After Globalization', *Third Text* 26:5 (2012): 515-527.

Léger, Marc James. 'The Subject Supposed to Over-Identify: BAVO and the Fundamental Fantasy of a Cultural Avant Garde', in Léger (ed.) *Brave New Avant Garde: Essays on Contemporary Art and Politics*, Winchester, UK: Zero Books, 2012.

Raunig, Gerald, Gene Ray and Ulf Wuggenig (eds). *Critique of Creativity: Precarity, Subjectivity and Resistance in the 'Creative Industries'*, London: MayFly Books, 2011.

Roberts, John. 'Art, "Enclave Theory" and the Communist Imaginary', *Third Text* 23:4 (2009): 353-367.

Sholette, Gregory. *Dark Matter: Art and Politics in the Age of Enterprise Culture*, London: Pluto, 2011.

Yúdice, George. *The Expediency of Culture: Uses of Culture in the Global Era*, Durham: Duke University Press, 2003.

Žižek, Slavoj. *The Fragile Absolute, or, Why Is the Christian Legacy Worth Fighting For?*, London: Verso, 2000.

Žižek, Slavoj. *Less than Nothing: Hegel and the Shadow of Dialectical Materialism*, London: Verso, 2012.

THE ART OF NEW CLASS GEOGRAPHY OF THE CITY: CULTURE-GUIDED URBAN REGENERATION SERVING THE MODERNIZATION OF THE PERIPHERY

ANA VILENICA

This text was written within the framework of the project 'Creative Work and Urban Regenerations', financed by the Secretariat for Science and Technological Development of the Autonomous Province of Vojvodina, as part of a campaign entitled 'The Right to a First Chance'. One version of this text was published in a collection of papers of the Institute for Researching Art in Novi Sad: Vilenica, Ana, 'Umetnost regeneracije gra-da—Predu(z)metništvo kao biznis model novih geopolitičkih konstelacija [The Art of City Regeneration: Artepreneurship as a Business Model of New Geopolitical Constellations]'.

The capitalization of cultural resources has become a central issue of post-industrial urban rule, and in capitalist societies art and culture has become an important instrument in the processes of creating new spatial and geopolitical constellations. Creative armies of designers and artists are employed as a resource for cosmetic renovations of cities, production of simulacra of authenticity and symbolic capital in the process of creating a new class geography of the city. In the context of Serbia, such a structural connection between culture, art and capital is practiced within the framework of the project of *cultivating* the capitalist periphery through the practices of culture-guided urban regenerations wherein the art establishment, cultural and creative industries and social-entrepreneurial art take part. In the local context, culture-guided urban regenerations are most often presented uncritically, as an always positive contribution of the processes of city *development,* the shaping of its *identity,* its *modernization* and *progress,* both in public narratives and in the academic discourse. Such a discursive practice acts as an accomplice to the attempts at smoothly carrying out aggressive processes of transformation in cities that merely continue to produce the unendurable state of enormous social disparities, the degradation of workers' and social rights and the environment, as well as the all-round discrimination of all those who do not belong to the desirable higher classes, ethnicity, race or sexual orientation. Understanding this state of affairs, as well as the role of culture and art, in a situation of constant production of manipulative images and false promises, turns out to be an important perspective towards articulating possible future forms of struggle and creation of 'new territories'.[1]

---

1   Raúl Zibechi, *Territories in Resistance: A Cartography of Latin American Social Movements,* Edinburgh: AK Press, 2012.

Urban Regenerations and the Role of Art and Culture

In capitalist societies, the connection between art and urban regenerations is established as a model of producing a new class geography of the city.[2] Such connections have been made possible through the interpenetration of art and the entire social and cultural production mechanism under the conditions of the cultural colonization of life effected by capitalist production.[3] Under these circumstances, art has become a resource and one of the important places when it comes to constructing power. The historical genesis of the connection between art and the transformation of cities is linked to the context of the USA and the 1970's, when art created the preconditions for the increase of real estate prices in reindustrialized cities[4] and thus for a new class recomposition of the city. In the districts where artists came to live, art studios and art galleries proliferated, and their symbolic capital increased the level of the rent, so that poorer inhabitants of such districts tended to move out, and were eventually followed by the artists themselves, who were replaced by richer city dwellers. Today, the processes of class recomposition of cities have been generalized at the global level, and their mechanisms include manipulating *collective symbolic capital* as a new apparatus of capitalist accumulation.[5]

In the local context, the establishment of connections between art and urban regenerations became possible with the forcible transformation of socialist Yugoslavia after the 1990s and the establishment of new capitalist relations. This change was accompanied by the wartime destruction of cities—urbicide, the transformation of ownership structure from social to private ownership, the switch from self-management relations to capitalist-exploitative relations, the development of corruption mechanisms and the absence of regulations when it came to the acquisition of capital, deindustrialization, the pauperization of the population, as well as the destruction of the existing mechanisms for work in the domain of culture and art, and the implementation of a new art/entrepreneurial model. In the era of socialism, the development of cities was based on central urban

---

2   David Harvey, *Rebel Cities: From the Right to the City to the Urban Revolution*, London: Verso, 2012; Josephine Berry Slater and Anthony Iles, *No Room to Move: Radical Art and Regenerate City*, London: Mute, 2010; Matteo Pasquinelli, 'Kreativna sabotaža u fabrici kulture: umetnost, džentrifikacija i metropola [Creative Sabotage in the Culture Factory: Art, Gentrification and the Metropolis], in Ana Vilenica and kuda.org. *Na ruševinama kreativnog grada*, Novi Sad: kuda.org, 2012.

3   Fredric Jameson, *Postmodernizam u kasnom kapitalizmu* [*Postmodernism in Late Capitalism*], Belgrade: KIZ Art Press, 1995; Ana Vilenica, *Teorije i prakse aktivizma u umetnosti u drugoj polovini XX veka* [*Theories and Practices of Activism in Art in the Second Half of the 20th Century*], PhD thesis, The University of the Arts, University of Belgrade, 2012.

4   Rosalyn Deutsche and Gandel Cara Rian, 'The Fine Art of Gentrification', *October* 31 (Winter, 1984): 91-111.

5   David Harvey, *Rebel Cities*.

planning, and the state was the chief investor and planner of the new modern socialist city, aimed at fulfilling the needs of the new socialist man. Today, the new initiators of *urban development* are private and corporate investors, acting in cooperation with the state, city administration, global financial institutions, civil society organizations, and also with artists and workers in the sphere of culture.[6] This kind of *investor planning* is characterized by a continual search for a profitable terrain where a surplus of value can be achieved, which is controlled by particular elites. In such a situation, urban regenerations no longer represent merely an act of repairing the neglected parts of the city, but most often constitute a radical act of pulling down the existing buildings and building new ones. Such processes are no longer a part of systematic thinking about cities. The idea and role of a general urban planning design almost matter not at all, for an investor who purchases a cheap plot of land, having previously deliberately lowered the building costs, will not have any great difficulties when it comes to changing the regulated function of that particular area. In this way, the city stops being a space where one strives to establish at least a nominal equality of its inhabitants, and becomes a space of drastic social and economic inequalities and tensions. The development of cities is promoted through new optimistic visions promising benefits for all. This urban optimism simultaneously hides the process of the creation of new class topography of the city, and a revengeful attitude towards those inhabitants who are not among the privileged ones.[7]

Art and culture become an instrument and accomplices in such processes through the inclusion of creativity as applied imagination in the processes of producing optimistic urban visions. That is what metanarratives about creative industries, creative cities and creative economy are all about.[8] In these narratives, culture and art are reduced to their economic function in the project of attracting investors, tourism and stimulating the economy through a reduction of labor costs and social contributions, giving a boost to the entrepreneurial model of work, privatization of culture and maximizing profit. On the one hand, it is an urban mantra, and on the other, it constitutes a social-economic and cultural policy. What is at work here is a complex mechanism that absorbs all the aspects of life in exercising control and exploitation in cities. In the local context and in other so-called transitional societies, the introduction of the cultural industry and the implementation of ideas about creative economy and creative city are viewed as an act of modernizing a *backward* society. The insufficient presence of such practices is explained by the incompatibility of the administrative, legal, banking and business systems in post-

---

6   Ana Vilenica and kuda.org, 'Preuzmimo grad! Kako? [Let's Take Over the City! How?], in Vilenica, Ana, kuda.org, *Na ruševinama kreativnog grada*, Novi Sad: kuda.org, 2012.

7   Neil Smith, *New Urban Frontier: Gentrification and the Revanchist City*, London: Routledge, 1996.

8   Richard Florida, *Cities and the Creative Class*, London: Routledge, 2005; UN CER. United Nations Creative Economy Report (UN CER), United Nations, 2008, http://unctad.org/en/Docs/ditc20082cer_en.pdf; Nada Švob-Đokić (ed.) *The Emerging Creative industries in Southeastern Europe*, Zagreb: Institute for International Relations, 2005.

socialist countries with those of 'advanced economies'.[9] In countries of South-Eastern Europe, this *modernization model* is implemented through state policies, the policies of cultural institutions and missions such as the British Council or the Goethe Institute, and also as a business strategy of private investors. Thus big cities in Serbia are regenerated through European and local *policies* about creative cities, such as the *Belgradisation of Belgrade* project and Belgrade's bid for a European Capital of Culture in 2020,[10] as well as the latest EU cultural project entitled *Creative Europe*. Also, regeneration is carried out by organizing cultural, entertainment or sports events such as the *Universiade* or the *Eurovision Song Contest*, and through individual projects promoting cultural indus-tries and art as a generator of urban regeneration processes[11] and a guarantor of social inclusion in their implementation. Such practices are aimed at creating an image of the city as an innovative, exciting, creative and safe place for living, playing and consump-tion, promising benefits for all, whereas what is, in fact, being planned is a city of walled fortresses wherein the elite and its way of life are to be reproduced.

In the local context, since the 1990's culture and art have become an instrument of *pro-gressive EU policies* aimed at creating an environment conducive to effecting a transition to neoliberal capitalism by way of carrying out the so-called *democratization of culture*, the proclaimed goal of which was to free art and culture from the patronage of the state and the Party, as a system which, allegedly, *a priori* jeopardizes the basic human rights and the potential for creative expression of individuals. What was produced in this pro-cess was a new entrepreneurial subject of the artist, one no longer protected through public financing but struggling for him/herself on the market.[12] In this way, art was used as a convenient tool for *cultivating* people on the capitalist periphery. This neo-colonial process has not been finished yet. Today, it is reproduced in the sphere of the imple-mentation of cultural industries and social-entrepreneurial art used in the project of a *new modernization* of local society, which is viewed as backward, and is particularly in evidence in the cases of instrumentalization of art in the processes of urban regenera-tions. A new profile of the artist that is promoted in this way is the entrepreneurial artist-artepreneur[13] who resolves problems in a non-linear and creative manner. He/she is a

---

9   Inga Tomić-Koludrović, Mirko Petrić, 'Creative Industries in Transition: Towards a Creative Economy?', in Nada Švob-Đokić (ed.), *The Emerging Creative industries in Southeastern Europe*.

10   Vida Knežević, Marko Miletić, 'Beograd 2020: Grad čuda, nova kulturna politika u Srbiji i prostori borbe [Belgrade 2020: A City of Wonder, the New Cultural Policy in Serbia and the Spaces of Struggle]' in Ana Vilenica, kuda.org, *Na ruševinama kreativnog grada* [*On the Ruins of the Creative City*], Novi Sad: kuda.org, 2012.

11   Vilenica and kuda.org, 'Preuzmimo grad! Kako? [Let's Take Over the City! How?]'.

12   Dušan Grlja, 'Antinomies of Post-Socialist Autonomy', *Red Thread*, 2009, http://www.red-thread. org/en/article.asp?a=16.

13   Pierre Guillet de Monthoux, 'Organising Reality Machines: Artepreneurs and the New Aesthetic Enlightenment', in Daniel Hjorth (ed.), *Handbook on Organisational Entrepreneurship*,

precarious worker who manages his/her human capital through self-employment from one project to another. The figure of artepreneur assumes a particularly important role in times of crisis, when it emerges, on the one hand, as a victim of the macroeconomic situation, and on the other, as a force that brings salvation.[14] In contemporary art, the very idea of emancipation and activism has become an issue related to entrepreneurship, and thereby, being placed in the service of capital, normalized to a great extent.

Art-guided Urban Regenerations in Belgrade

In Serbia, culture- and art-guided urban regenerations have been promoted over the course of the past decade, and the realization of such ideas has only intensified in the last few years. We find examples of practices of culture- and art-guided urban regenerations in Serbia in big cities, mostly in Belgrade, where the political, economic and cultural life of Serbia is centralized. The epicenter of such activities is in the area of Belgrade's riverbanks, which is currently the most exclusive and profitable location in Belgrade. There has been interest in the areas on the banks of the Sava and Danube rivers for a number of years, and various projects prepared for that part of the city have reflected the political, economic and cultural climate in the newly established state. In early 1990, the Serbian Academy of Sciences and Arts called an internal tender, within the framework of which the project 'Water City' emerged, and in 1996 the Socialist Party of Serbia commissioned the project *Europolis*.[15] These projects have never been realized, but that part of the city has never stopped attracting the attention of new investors and the political parties in power, most often during the course of pre-election campaigns.

The interest shown in Belgrade's riverbanks is not accidental and does not concern only the attractiveness of the actual location. It also has to do with the systematic work aimed at creating a new identity for Serbia and Belgrade, in a place which, during the pre-socialist period, in the first half of the 19th century, was projected to become the economic centre of the city.[16] It was there that the history of capitalist Serbia was made, aiming to establish a continuity through a systematic erasure of the socialist history and the industrial development of this area. What is worrying about this is the fact that this old Belgrade was a city of enormous class differences, where more than 80% of the

Northampton: Edward Elgar, 2012.

14   Campbell Jones and Anna-Maria Murtola, 'Entrepreneurship, Crisis, Critique', in Daniel Hjorth (ed.), *Handbook on Organisational Entrepreneurship.*

15   'Beograd na vodi ili političari u kampanji [Belgrade on Water or Politicians Campaigning], *Politika*, 11 August 2013, http://www.politika.rs/rubrike/Beograd/Beograd-na-vodi-ili-politicari-u-kampanji. lt.html.

16   Miloš Jovanović, *Constructing the National Capital*, master diss., CEU, Budapest, 2008.

population lived in extreme poverty.[17] The riverbanks are also a place of memory engineering, connected with the recent history of the wars fought in the 1990's on the territory of the former Yugoslavia, which represents a continuation of the processes of historical revisionism in Serbia, without which a projection of Belgrade as a new European-Serbian urban centre for the higher classes is not possible. One of the first great state projects of the regeneration of that area was the renovation of Sava Square[18], which began by the expulsion of female sexual workers from the area, whose place was taken over by a new revisionist monument to all war victims and defenders of the homeland in the 1990-1999 period, thus equating victims and executioners, and continuing the tradition of forgetting the fact that the role of Serbia in those wars was that of an aggressor.

Today, that profitable area has become a battlefield where two megaprojects vie for power: the project launched by the privately owned company the Port of Belgrade entitled *Water City*, and the project initiated by the Government of Serbia entitled *Belgrade on Water*. *Water City* is an elite settlement occupying an area of 96 hectares of land, whereas *Belgrade on Water* occupies a considerably larger area of around 950 hectares of land, for which, apart from housing, the building of business parks and a new port for yachts are also planned.[19] By planning the processes of urban regenerations and involving art and cultural industries in the local strategic plans, the new creators of optimistic visions wish to make Belgrade a part of the world market of cities and make up for the decline of economic activities in the city. The main social trump card of these projects is their promise to resolve the problem of unemployment by creating new jobs in the sphere of construction work during the realization phase, in the service sector of the new walled communities, and also in the sector of cultural industries, whereas what is happening in practice is a flexibilization and deregulation of the procedures for investors and undertakers, coupled with a degradation of workers' rights, which means an increasingly frantic exploitation of all those engaged on the projects. Experienced engineers of urban transformations, such as renowned world architects, as well as mayors of cities wherein such processes have been practiced, have already been involved in the initiation of urban regeneration processes through the projects *Water City* and *Belgrade on Water*. Thus the main designer of the *Water City* project is the studio of Daniel Libeskind, whose biography includes numerous projects through which similar processes have been initiated in other cities, and the main consultant of the *Belgrade on Water* project is the well-known New York mayor Rudolph Giuliani, whose brutal class and racist cleansing of New York in the 1990's is well known.[20] The initial phases of both projects involve the use of art

17   Zlata Vuksanović-Macura, *Život na ivici: Stanovanje sirotinje u Beogradu 1919-1941* [*Living on the Edge: The Housing of the Poor in Belgrade 1919-1941*], Belgrade: Orion Art, 2012.

18   'Uskoro novo lice Savskog trga [Soon, a New Look of Sava Square], *Blic*, 28 November 2011,

19   Večernje novosti, 14 October 2013, Politika, 11 August 2013, 'Water City': the Port of Belgrade, 2010.

20   Smith, 1996, Politika, 11 September 2012.

and cultural industries, which play the key role in the preparatory phase of changing the function of the area in question. They are a part of the marketing strategy for promoting its transformation, as well as a *guarantor of the social awareness* of new spatial transformations. These involve the projects *Soho in Belgrade, Mixer* and *Urban Incubator.*

The project 'Soho in Belgrade' was initiated by the Port of Belgrade company in 2012, as part of preparations for the realization of *Water City.* The project presupposed enabling artists with well-established reputations to use studios, free of charge, in one of the warehouses inside the port, located in Dunavska Street, which formerly belonged to the *Srbijateks* company. The aim of this joint initiative of tycoons and the art establishment was the creation of the so-called *Soho effect.* Over the past several years, this term has become a synonym for urban regenerations in a number of instances involving the relocation of art studios and artists' flats to derelict part of cities in the hope of producing additional symbolic capital and thus initiating the accumulation of capital. In the case of the project *Soho in Belgrade*, the bringing of artists to the warehouse had another function in addition to the aforementioned one, namely, participation in the process of changing the purpose of the space where the port operator is located.[21] What this is all about are the efforts of the *Worldfin* company to close down the port through a drastic reduction of its scope of business operations, and to effect a symbolic and legal change of its function, so as to be able to build a new luxury settlement on that plot of land. From the very start, the new owner wanted to hide the fact that, according to the general urban plan, that plot of land was designated to have an economic function, and that its privatization involved a port operator only. Through corruptive arrangements between political parties and tycoons, a change of the general urban plan was brought about, so that the function of that part of the city was changed from an economic one to a housing-commercial one. Further room for maneuvering was provided by the problem that arose over entering the city in the registry book as the owner of the said plot of land. To put it more precisely, the new owners made use of the fact that the city failed to observe the deadline and submitted incomplete documentation, and proclaimed that plot of land to be theirs. Apart from the change of the general urban plan, manipulation over entering the owner in the registry book and the reduction of the operative capacity of the port operator, art was also involved in the process of changing the function of that plot of land through the project *Soho in Belgrade.*

That artists are activists operating in the service of local tycoons is evidenced by the situation that arose after the Ministry of Infrastructure and Energy, acting upon a request submitted by the Anti-Corruption Council, passed a decision on evicting artists from the Port of Belgrade on account of irregularities in the procedure of allocating studios to artists. Artists from Soho mobilized themselves in defense of the owner of the Port,

21   Ana Vilenica, 'Soho u Beogradu: Umetnička elita u službi tajkuna [Soho in Belgrade: The Art Elite in the Service of Tycoons], in *Maribor 2012*, 14 September 2011, http://82.149.22.226/~mobcinamb/index.php?ptype=8&menu=0&id=220&Pid=617.

whom they presented to the public as a new patron of the arts who, as opposed to the state, provided artists with a *roof above their heads*.[22] It is a fact that the working conditions of artists, after the degradation of the socialist-era mechanisms that enabled artists to obtain a studio, had become almost unendurable. However, the artists in question here are not a part of the class of artists who do need help. These are successful artists-entrepreneurs, who are favorably positioned on the world art market, most of whom do have their own working space, whereas some of them do not live in Belgrade. These *Sohoite* artists constitute the embodiment of everything that the new art establishment represents today. These are positions that are defended through a return to aestheticism and individual expression as the main criterion of art. Within the framework of this kind of positioning, opportunism and commercialism become desirable characteristics and a generator of success. What is at work here is a reactionary artistic practice that is articulated in opposition to the domain of critical and contextual practices, with which it enters into an open conflict through its insistence on being separated from sociability as the measure of true art. In Belgrade's Soho, studios were allocated to select elite artists, without anything in the nature of a public competition, which resulted in the exclusion of those artists who are engaged in non-market-oriented artistic practices, who are dependent on public financing and who do need a working space. This resulted in an unbridgeable gap on the art scene, which became visible to the public when the *Sohoites* organized a panel discussion at the Kolarac People's University, in the course of which public interest was defended by a group of artists presenting themselves as *The World Communal Heritage*. [23]

To the present day, the artists in the service of tycoons have not been evicted from the studios in the *Srbijateks* warehouse, for the commission that is supposed to carry out their eviction has never inspected the site, which, once again, serves to hide the corruptive mechanisms in the state. The epilogue of the story about the Port of Belgrade commenced in August 2013, through the initiation of the bankruptcy procedure. Parallel with this, the Government of Serbia, through the representatives of the ruling Serbian Progressive Party, embarked on a new campaign of promoting the project *Belgrade on Water*.[24] It is important to point out that a part of the project *Belgrade on Water* is being planned on the plot of land held by the operator of the Port of Belgrade, which sheds more light on why the bankruptcy procedure is being initiated right now, despite the efforts of the Anti-Corruption Agency of many years to point out the irregularities surrounding the privatization and operation of that company. In this case, it would appear that the more powerful bureaucrats have used the tycoons to close down the port operations in order

---

22   Vilenica, 'Soho u Beogradu'.

23   Vilenica, 'Soho u Beogradu'.

24   'Pokrenut stečaj Luke Beograd [The Bankruptcy Procedure Initiated for the Port of Belgrade], *Vreme*, 6 August 2013, http://www.vreme.rs/cms/view.php?id=1130342.

to take over a part of the land already prepared for this purpose.

Even though the project *Belgrade on Water* was presented to the public only midway through 2013, systematic preparations for its implementation have been carried out for several years, by engaging art and cultural industries in the district which, by means of the fabrication of tradition, has become known again under the name of Savamala. The model of regeneration being implemented in Savamala today is based on an attempt to introduce a creative economy through creative industries, within the framework of a project of increasing the symbolic capital of the place and resolving the problem of economic deficit through *creativization* and artistic-communal-participatory-social entrepreneurship with a view to normalizing the situation of social dissatisfaction, as well as a new legitimization of the history of the place. These processes were not initiated by the city authorities but by *independent* cultural initiatives, in cooperation with business groups and with the German cultural mission—the Goethe Institute. Still, the city and municipal authorities support the initiatives undertaken through budget financing, allow-ing the use of space owned by the city, and through affirmation by means of projects of establishing creative economies and producing a creative city such as *Belgrade 2020*, which accompanies Belgrade's bid for a European Capital of Culture.

The introduction and affirmation of cultural industries and stimulation of the develop-ment of entrepreneurial creative economy as a form of social activism and struggle for the revitalization of Savamala is a task set by the project *Mixer,* which includes the eponymous festival and the newly opened venue *Mixer House.*[25] Even though *Mixer* pro-poses a model of partnership with the business sector, as a practice of the *de-etatization* of the creative sector and its *liberation,* in a parallel development public budget funds are invested in the project through a number of public companies and funds, which clearly shows a switch in the domain of public financing—from support given to critical practices to support given to commercial initiatives. The idea of *Mixer* is to turn Belgrade into a Balkan creative centre and incubator for young creative talents by developing the concept of the creative city with a nucleus in the industrial zone that is losing its func-tion. What is at work here are efforts aimed at the accumulation of symbolic capital in Savamala through the promotion of established creators and entertainers, and through a frantic exploitation of all those who are not privileged. The ethics of entrepreneurial inventiveness is used to hide the issue of the precarious work conditions of those who do not belong to the top echelon, their enforced volunteer work and the imposition of hierarchical models, and often the investment of the personal funds of young artists during the realization of works that are featured in the programs of 'Mixer'. On the other hand, 'Mixer' is also a form of incubator for producing an army of creative workers who are supposed to set the creative industry in motion, as a sphere that is broader than cultural industries, in the domain of a new urbanization of Belgrade. *Mixer* is deeply

25   Mikser [Mixer], 4 August 2013, http://blog.mikser.rs/o-mikseru.

involved in the processes of the so-called 'creative destruction [26] through initiating new mechanisms for the accumulation of capital in the course of paving the way for the arrival of investors and the building of *Water City*. It is one of those entrepreneurial tactics that glorifies the successes of individuals and neglects the failures of the majority, and instead of new social networks, it offers alienated consumerism. What is created in this way is a false promise of creating new *authentic* relations, paving the way for capitalist uniformity at all levels.

Parallel with *Mixer*, the processes of urban regenerations in Savamala are also initiated using a somewhat different method, through the practices of communal-participative-social art, as a subgroup of the creative sector, which are realized within the framework of the Goethe Institute project *Urban Incubator*.[27] *Urban Incubator* was presented as a participative model of urban development, whose aim is to improve the quality of life of the local population and to *democratize* the process of decision-making by means of a higher degree of involvement of the inhabitants of the district. The project is a short-term one, will last one year, and during that time it should accumulate symbolic capital and increase the market value of the district, following which the artists will withdraw, leaving room for the coming of investors and the development of tourism. *Urban Incubator* represents an attempt at implementing the *Western model* of culture-guided urban regeneration in the local context (of the eleven projects that were accepted in the competition, only two were initiated by local artists and architects), and has been recognized as such by the local city authorities and the municipality of Savski venac—as having potential for the *development* of Savamala.

Realizing projects within the framework of *Urban Incubator*, the artists engaged assume the competencies of urban planners, social workers, ethnographers and researchers, and pass themselves off as experts when it comes to reinventing the space of Savamala through interventions in public space, collecting personal stories from the community, participative design, *crowdsourcing*, designing small businesses and micro factories with a view to enlivening the area and engaging people from the local community in order to establish a continuity with the entrepreneurial history of the place. Such an artistic practice represents a specific architecture of the community that includes economic exchange, civic life, public property and the establishment of various new connections. What is evident about this project is that it privileges participative art as a tool for cosmetic interventions aimed at resolving the systemic problems of Savamala, or even resorting to enforced participation or imposing parameters of art projects onto the inhabitants of Savamala with the intention of 'beautifying their living space and increas-

---

26 Marshall Berman, *All That Is Solid Melts into Air: The Experience of Modernity*, Ringwood: Viking Penguin. 1988; David Harvey, *The Condition of Postmodernity*. Cambridge MA and Oxford UK: Blackwell, 1992.

27 Urban Incubator Belgrade, http://www.goethe.de/ins/cs/bel/prj/uic/enindex.htm.

ing the market value of their flats'.[28] This coupling points to the ideological subtext of participative-social-entrepreneurial artistic practices, which can be defined as a *culturalization of politics* or a dislocation of discourse on complex and provocative social and political topics into the sphere of culture and art.[29] 'Urban Incubator' is a symptom of social architects' *paranoid fear* of social unrest, and they engage art as a *dependable means* of pacifying the accumulated dissatisfaction of the inhabitants of Savamala, offering them a promise of a better life, all the while, in fact, paving the way for the arrival of real estate traders and opening more and more nightclubs and cafés.

Conclusion

The transformation of the existing socialist structures and mechanisms of cultural and artistic production, as well as the abandonment of certain projects of sociability, the diminishing and increasingly non-transparent public financing and the devastation of cultural institutions, as well as giving in to the operation of the market forces, have created conditions that are unendurable for the vast majority of artists and workers in the sphere of culture. Seemingly paradoxically, the public and investors give their support to the art establishment and initiatives that promote *apolitical* entrepreneurial artistic-designer practices. The creation of such conditions has produced a fertile soil for manipulation and instrumentalization of art by the state and its powerful bureaucrats, tycoons and their firms and corporations, the cultural missions of national European states and the broader EU policies, as well as local cultural entrepreneurs who believe that they are on their way to becoming capitalists.

As has been shown in the local context and in countries of the periphery, what is at work here is practicing certain creative-economic models of regeneration of cities in the name of the *modernization* and *democratization* of local society and its economy, within the framework of which are intertwined *national and neo-colonial modernization*, which act as accomplices in the process of producing the spaces of capitalist periphery. What this is about is the implementation of new neoliberal regimes of producing cities and creating conditions for producing a new class geography in spaces where there are still populations of different social and economic status living together, and, naturally enough, the production of new mechanisms of flexibilization of work and legislation in a project wherein the local environment continues to be produced as a resource for *the developed world*, and which is kept under control by means of carefully measured loans which create a condition of *debt slavery*. Through the use of art, culture and the cultural industry, *Western models* of urban regenerations are implemented, the intention being

---

28 C5, School of Urban Practices, http://projectc5.blogspot.it/ (http://www.academia.edu/771895/On_participatory_art_Interview_with_Claire_Bishop).

29 George Yudice, *The Expediency of Culture: Uses of Culture in the Global Era*, Durham and London: Duke University Press, 2003.

to produce a quick effect of changing the function of the given space, increasing its symbolic capital, producing a new *identity* of the city, introducing new forms of capitalist economy, as well as normalizing potential social conflicts.

Still, despite their above-mentioned instrumental function in the processes of reshaping cities, art, creativity and culture can also represent significant factors of the destabilization of such *smooth* processes of capital-guided urban transformation, and can participate in producing a city based on different and more egalitarian relations, outside the proven exploitative relations of power and division of labor. For them to be established as such, it is necessary, to begin with, to articulate a radical class critique of the (newly established) capitalist relations in formerly socialist cities in Serbia, as well as a critique of the use of art and culture, and also to be engaged in continual theoretical-activistic-political work on producing different relations, which are anxiously articulated today through certain local practices in a state of *insobriety* produced by the social transformation and the new rules of the game wherein (artistic and cultural) activism becomes an instrument of capital.

References

Barok, Dušan. *On Participatory Art: Interview with Clear Bishop.* Prague: Transit Initiative, 29 July 2009, *http://www.academia.edu/771895/On_participatory_art_Interview_with_Claire_Bishop* (http://www.academia.edu/771895/On_participatory_art_Interview_with_Claire_Bishop).

Berman, Marshall (http://en.wikipedia.org/wiki/Marshall_Berman). *All That Is Solid Melts into Air: The Experience of Modernity* (http://books.google.co.uk/books?id=mox1ywiyhtgC), Ringwood: Viking Penguin. 1988.

Beograd 2020. *http://www.beograd2020.com/* (http://www.beograd2020.com/).

Beograd na vodi: projekat vredan osam milijardi evra! [Belgrade on Water: A Project Worth Eight Billion Euros!], *Večernje novosti*, 14 October 2013, *http://www.kurir-info.rs/beograd-na-vodi-projekat-vredan-osam-milijardi-evra-clanak-1034045* (http://www.kurir-info.rs/beograd-na-vodi-projekat-vredan-osam-milijardi-evra-clanak-1034045).

Beograd na vodi ili političari u kampanji [Belgrade on Water or Politicians Campaigning], *Politika*, 11 August 2013, *http://www.politika.rs/rubrike/Beograd/Beograd-na-vodi-ili-politicari-u-kampanji.lt.html* (http://www.politika.rs/rubrike/Beograd/Beograd-na-vodi-ili-politicari-u-kampanji.lt.html).

Berry Slater, J. and Iles, A. *No Room to Move: Radical Art and Regenerate City*, London: Mute, 2010.

C5, School of Urban Practices. *http://projectc5.blogspot.it/*(http://projectc5.blogspot.it/).

Creative Europe. http://ec.europa.eu/culture/creative-europe/(http://ec.europa.eu/culture/creative-europe/).

Dave Beech, 'Include Me Out!'. *ViS*, 1 September 2010, *http://visualintosocial.wordpress.com/category/talks/dave-beech-on-participation/*(http://visualintosocial.wordpress.com/category/talks/dave-beech-on-participation/).

Castells, Manuel. *The Urban Question*, London: Edward Arnold, 1977.

Deutsche, Rosalyn and Cara Gandel Rian. 'The fine art of gentrification', *October* 31 (Winter,

1984): 91-111.

Foster, Hal. *The Return of the Real*, Massachusetts: MIT Press, 1996.

Florida, Richard. *Cities and the Creative Class*, London: Routledge, 2005.

Florida, Richard. *The Rise of the Creative Class and how it's Transforming Work, Leisure and Everyday Life*, London: Basic Books, 2002.

Glass, Ruth. *London: Aspects of Change*, London: Centre for Urban Studies, 1964.

Grad na vodi: Luka Beograd [Water City: the Port of Belgrade], *http://www.lukabeograd.com/ GradNaVodi/Masterplan.html*(http://www.lukabeograd.com/GradNaVodi/Masterplan.html).

Grlja, Dušan. 'Antinomies of Post-Socialist Autonomy'. *Red Thread* (2009), *http://www.red-thread. org/en/article.asp?a=16* (http://www.red-thread.org/en/article.asp?a=16).

Harvey, David. *The Urbanization of Capital*. Oxford: Basil Blackwell, 1985.

Harvey, David. *The Condition of Postmodernity*. Cambridge MA and Oxford UK: Blackwell, 1992.

Harvey David. *Rebel Cities: From the Right to the City to the Urban Revolution*, London: Verso, 2012.

Incident na otkrivanju spomenika na Savskom trgu [Incident During the Unveiling of the Monument in Sava Square], *Kurir*, 24 March 2012.

Jameson, Fredric. *Postmodernizam u kasnom kapitalizmu* [*Postmodernism in Late Capitalism*], Belgrade: KIZ Art Press, 1995.

Jones, Campbell and Murtola, Anna-Maria. 'Entrepreneurship, Crisis, Critique, in Hjorth, Daniel (ed.) *Handbook on Organisational Entrepreneurship*, Edward Elgar: Northampton, 2012.

Jovanović, Miloš. *Constructing the National Capital*, master diss., CEU Budapest, 2008.

Knežević, Vida, Miletić, Marko. 'Beograd 2020: Grad čuda, nova kulturna politika u Srbiji i prostori borbe [*Belgrade 2020: A City of Wonder, the New Cultural Policy in Serbia and the Spaces of Struggle*], in Ana Vilenica and kuda.org *Na ruševinama kreativnog grada* [*On the Ruins of the Creative City*], Novi Sad: kuda.org, 2012.

Libby Porter and Kate Shaw (eds). *Whose Urban Renaissance*, London: Routledge, 2009.

Luka Beograd. Grad na vodi [The Port of Belgrade – Water City], http://www.lukabeograd.com/ GradNaVodi/Masterplan.html.

Mikser [Mixer]. *http://blog.mikser.rs/o-mikseru. 04th August 2013*(http://blog.mikser.rs/o-mikseru.%2004.%20avgust%202013).

Monthoux, Pierre Guillet de. 'Organising Reality Machines: Artepreneurs and the new Aesthetic Enlightenment', in Daniel Hjorth (ed.), *Handbook on Organisational Entrepreneurship*, Northampton: Edward Elgar, 2012.

Pasquinelli, Matteo. 'Kreativna sabotaža u fabrici kulture: umetnost, džentrifikacija i metropola [Creative Sabotage in the Culture Factory: Art, Gentrification and the Metropolis], in Ana Vilenica and kuda.org. *Na ruševinama kreativnog grada*, Novi Sad: kuda.org, 2012.

Peck, Jamie. 'The Creativity Fix' in *Eurozine*, 28 June 2007, http://www.eurozine.com/ articles/2007-06-28-peck-en.html.

Pokrenut stečaj Luke Beograd [The Bankruptcy Procedure Initiated for the Port of Belgrade], *Vreme*, 6 August 2013, *http://www.vreme.rs/cms/view.php?id=1130342* (http://www.vreme.rs/ cms/view.php?id=1130342)

Počela beogradizacija Beograda [The Belgradisation of Belgrade Begins], *Blic*, 2 August 2010,

http://www.blic.rs/Vesti/Beograd/201025/Pocela-Beogradizacija-Beograda (http://www.blic.rs/
Vesti/Beograd/201025/Pocela-Beogradizacija-Beograda).

Rikalović, Gojko. *Kreativna Srbija: Novi pravci razvoja* [*Creative Serbia: New Directions of Development*]. Belgrade: Anonymous said, 2011.

Rudolf Džulijani u poseti Beogradu i SNS [Rudolph Giuliani Visits Belgrade and the Serbian Progressive Party], *Politika*, 11 September 2012.

Soho u Beogradu [Soho in Belgrade], *http://www2.lukabeograd.com/soho-bg.html*(http://www2.lukabeograd.com/soho-bg.html).

Smith, Neil. *Uneven Development: Nature, Capital, and the Production of Space*, Oxford: Basil Blackwell, 1990.

Smith, Neil. *New Urban Frontier: Gentrification and the Revanchist City*. London: Routledge, 1996.

Švob-Đokić, Nada (ed.). *The Emerging Creative industries in Southeastern Europe*, Zagreb: Institute for International Relations, 2005.

Tomić-Koludrović, Inga and Petrić, Mirko 'Creative Industries in Transition: Towards a Creative Economy?', in Švob-Đokić, Nada (ed.), *The Emerging Creative industries in Southeastern Europe*, Zagreb: Institute for International Relations, 2005.

UN CER. United Nations Creative Economy Report (UN CER), United Nations, 2008, *http://unctad.org/en/Docs/ditc20082cer_en.pdf* (http://unctad.org/en/Docs/ditc20082cer_en.pdf).

Urban Incubator Belgrade, *http://www.goethe.de/ins/cs/bel/prj/uic/enindex.htm* (http://www.goethe.de/ins/cs/bel/prj/uic/enindex.htm).

Uskoro novo lice Savskog trga [Soon, a New Look of Sava Square], *Blic*, 28 November 2011.

Vilenica, Ana. *Teorije i prakse aktivizma u umetnosti u drugoj polovini XX veka* [*Theories and Practices of Activism in Art in the Second Half of the 20th Century*], PhD thesis, The University of the Arts, University of Belgrade, 2012.

Vilenica, Ana and kuda.org. 'Preuzmimo grad! Kako? [Let's Take Over the City! How?], in Vilenica, Ana, kuda.org, *Na ruševinama kreativnog grada*, Novi Sad: kuda.org, 2012.

Vilenica, Ana. 'Soho u Beogradu: Umetnička elita u službi tajkuna [Soho in Belgrade: The Art Elite in the Service of Tycoons], in nsparentnost *2012*, 14 September 2011, http://82.149.22.226/~mobcinamb/index.php?ptype=8&menu=0&id=220&Pid=617.

Vuksanović-Macura, Zlata. *Život na ivici: Stanovanje sirotinje u Beogradu 1919-1941* [*Living on the Edge: The Housing of the Poor in Belgrade 1919-1941*], Belgrade: Orion Art, 2012.

World Bank. *Entrepreneurship Snapshots 2010: Measuring the Impact of the Financial Crisis on New Business Registration*, 2011.

Yudice, George. *The Expediency of Culture: Uses of Culture in the Global Era*, Durham and London: Duke University Press, 2003.

Zibechi, Raúl. *Territories in Resistance: A Cartography of Latin American Social Movements*, Edinburgh: AK Press, 2012.

Zukin, Sheron. *Cultures of the Cities*, Cambridge MA and Oxford UK: Blackwell, 1995.

Šeik 'doneo' BG na vodi, kredite... [The Sheikh 'Brings' Belgrade on Water, Loans], *B92*, 12 December 2013, http://www.b92.net/biz/vesti/srbija.php?yyyy=2013&mm=12&dd=12&nav_id=788601 (http://www.b92.net/biz/vesti/srbija.php?yyyy=2013&mm=12&dd=12&nav_id=788601).

THE CREATIVE FACTORY: COLLECTIVE CREATIVITY AND AUTONOMY IN THE NEOLIBERAL MACHINE OF CREATIVE INDUSTRIES

SANDI ABRAM

Introduction: Genteel Capital Courtship

A maxim constantly repeated by the Ljubljana Mayor in the last few years has been 'Ljubljana—the most beautiful city in the world'. The sentence condenses the dominant urbanistic managerial ideology of the Municipality of Ljubljana (hereafter MOL): the ideology of consumerist attractiveness. The grandiose urban plans following this directive are transforming the city into a postcard in order to send it and sell it, especially to the urban tourism industry which clings to the public image-making as well as to other formations of capital. The straightjacketing of the public space into lucrative, sterile, and disciplinary logic is not anything new. Yet some strategies of the neoliberal urbanism in city espoused with the reproduction of capital seem to be the new ones. Whereas the cultural consumption was fuelling the city's symbolic economy[1] for quite a while, the cities in the 21st century strain themselves to become areas of peculiar multifaceted production closely intertwined with consumption once again. This time they are shaping a pervasive marketing coalition between the cultural and art establishments, real estate speculators, service business, and city councils.

The contemporary urban tourism industry ceases to have the privileged sole position of the producer of surplus value in the metropolis. Instead, the neoliberal capital colonization is invading new spheres and ways of surplus extraction, while mimicking the ideological processes of gentrification under 'new planetary vulgates,'[2] such as the territorial 'creative milieu'[3] or the metropolitan 'creative city.'[4] The proponents of such 'new urban economy'[5] tend to blindly follow Florida's nostrum of the new paradigm for urban planning that can be found his all-encompassing predicament: 'Human creativity is the

---

1   Sharon Zukin, *Landscapes of Power: From Detroit to Disney World.* Berkeley: University of California Press, 1991. Sharon Zukin, *The Cultures of Cities,* Cambridge: Blackwell, 1995.

2   Pierre Bourdieu and Loïc Wacquant, 'NewLiberalSpeak. Notes on the new planetary vulgate', *Radical Philosophy* 105 (2001): 1-5.

3   Charles Landry, *The Creative City: A Toolkit for Urban Innovators,* London: Earthscan, 2000.

4   Richard Florida, *Cities and the Creative Class,* London, New York: Routledge, 2005.

5   Saskia Sassen, 'Locating cities on global circuits,' *Environment & Urbanization* 14 (2002): 22. http://www.rrojasdatabank.info/urban/euv14n1p13.pdf

ultimate source of economic growth.'[6] The territorial intertwines with the cognitive colonization only to become a situated 'creative economy' in the era of cognitive capitalism.

We can witness the entire trajectory of these processes through the case of a former bicycle factory in Ljubljana. Located in immediate vicinity of the city centre, the Rog factory operated until 1991, then remained closed and abandoned until 2006,[7] when, after 15 long years of stagnation, the group TEMP, along with a conglomerate of other praxes and realities,[8] reclaimed the factory for temporary use and brought the Fordist Frankenstein back to life. From 2010 onwards, the reappropriation of the commons was claimed. Ever since their liberation and reanimation, the spaces in Rog[2] present an open cultural, social, and political hub giving shelter to a multitude of autonomous collective political subjects[9] as well as to a broad range of artists and sports enthusiasts practicing horizontal organization and communication on a daily basis.

In order to demonstrate how the paradigmatic shift to postfordist cognitive capitalism is taking place and form in Ljubljana, I divided the article into three sections. It starts by introducing the project based on a public-private partnership bearing the name *Second Chance,* then highlighting its initial intentions with the autonomous Rog and the neoliberal discourse while advocating creative industries, urban regeneration etc. After problematizing the premises of the 'new urban economy' and of the designed emplacement of cognitive capitalism, the article focuses on pilot project RogLab which is seen as a pervasive creation of creative industries installed in the interim phase between the unveiling of the megalomaniac plans and their implementation by the owner of the factory, MOL. The third and concluding instance deals with the changed spatial design, showing the proposed publically financed gradual construction, or rather demolition, of the liberated Rog factory which has, in fact, the purpose of neutralization and eradication of the autonomous collective creativity in Rog, giving space to gentrification.

---

6   Richard Florida, *Cities and the Creative Class,* London, New York: Routledge, 2005, p. 22.

7   For a more detailed history of Rog from the second part of the 19th century onwards see Mihelič et al. (1995) or the historical digest available on Tovarna Rog website (http://tovarna.org/node/131); for a sociopolitical analysis see Kurnik and Beznec (2009); Kurnik (2013).

8   Cf. TEMP. 'TEMP about TEMP, or a quick and unsystematic retrospective of the workings of one temporary and informal multidisciplinary group.' In: Radical Education Collective (eds.): *New public spaces: dissensual political and artistic practices in the post-Yugoslav context,* Maastricht: Jan van Eyck Academie (2009): 144-158. Internet source: http://radical.temp.si/reader/TEMP.pdf

9   To name some: *Invisible Workers of the World, World for Everyone, Civil Initiative of the Erased Activists, Front of the Precarious, Iz-hod* (Walk-out) movement for the deinstitutionalization from total institutions, Occupy Movement #15o, Anti-Capitalist Block etc.

The Public-Private Partnership Model as a Pan-European Paradigm of Gentrification: Second Chance

Starting with the year 2010, MOL's endeavour to castrate Rog was wrapped inside a benevolent cellophane, launched under the name the Second Chance. The former Rog factory joined other postindustrial sites including the former AEG factory (Nuremberg), HALLE 14 of the former Cotton Spinning Mill (Leipzig), the tram depot (Krakow) and the Arsenale (Venice). In order to understand the vulgar slogan of *Second Chance* 'from industrial use to creative impulse' we shall dwell directly on the project's description:

> [The slogan] [i]t is a vision of five European cities to transform a disused industrial site into a cultural and creative work and living space and continuing their revitaliza-tion with sustainable concepts. [...] Nuremberg, Leipzig, Venice, Krakow and Ljubljana work together[10] to develop innovative strategies and concepts to upgrade their former industrial site to a key cultural linchpin of the city's district. The cities face the same challenges of developing a heritage and former industrial sites. Even though the revitalization process is at different stages in the five cities, the partners share the same questions, challenges, opportunities and goals. [...][11]

According to the initial plan, and through the private-public partnership model, the build-ings would be levelled first to the ground, and then, once the ruins were cleaned up, the Centre of Contemporary Arts was to be planned on top. To complement this grotesque picture, the entire Rog's surface (around 7,000 square meter) was to be split into private (80.69%) and public (19.31%) ownership, whereby the private 'content' would comprise a residential (apartments, underground garages), hotel and business section, while the public part were to be exclusively reserved for *creative industries* (multi-purpose halls, exhibition surfaces, studios etc.).[12] The logic behind the two bedfellows under neoliberal-ism is that the public would finance the private and the private would parasite on public benefits. The ideological premises nesting in the plan were in the apparent satisfaction of both sectors: the private sector with profit-making spaces and pseudopublic spaces as non-profit contents were to be designed for the public.

However, the unveiled case of the expropriation of the commons is far from being sat-isfactory. It is necessary to scale the whole problem on the level of new urban regime

---

10   Together work, of course, the city managers and the appurtenant administration.

11   Second Chance, *Project Description* (2013), pp. 4, http://www.secondchanceproject.eu/wp/?page_id=26

12   Institute for Civilisation and Culture. *SWOT Analysis for the Purposes of the Revitalisation of the Former Rog Factory with the Establishment of the Rog—Centre of Contemporary Arts* (2011). Internet source: http://www.secondchanceproject.eu/wp/wp-content/uploads/2011/07/SWOT_Analysis_Ljubljana.pdf

which does not necessarily cling any longer on the art world, as it symptomatically pro-
poses to erect the Centre of Contemporary Arts as well as spaces for arts and culture
to be featured inside. To expand a Hannah Arendt's thought into the milieu of 'creative
capitalism', the privatization of the public *and* the commons is intimately connected to
the privatization of the political. And to put it differently, gentrification through art was
complemented with the gentrification through 'creativity'. The culturalization of capital
under a new panacea for post-industrial sites means: creative 'revitalization through
arts and culture'.[13]

Generally speaking, gentrification can manifest in three forms: traditional, modern, and
artificial.[14] The traditional one is produced by exploiting historical and social 'guardians
of collective symbolic and cultural capital (the museums, the universities, the class of
benefactors, and the state apparatus)'.[15] The modern one is produced by exploiting the
art world and urban subcultures as the artificial gentrification is a strategy generated
by city councils through public campaigns which promote the creative city in order to
attract investments and highly skilled workers.[16] Concomitantly, the '[q]uality of urban
life has become a commodity, as has the city itself, in a world where consumerism, tourism, cultural and knowledge-based industries have become major aspects of the urban
political economy'.[17]

What remains overshadowed is the mode of accumulation of the *collective symbolic
capital*. This capital, after Slovenia's transition to neoliberalism, was not exploited due
to MOL's active negation of the autonomous cultural production in Rog today. In this
sense, neither squatters nor artists or other users of the postindustrial Rog had the role
of 'bridge gentrifiers'[18], i.e. transitional tenants, who would be tolerated only until they
raised property value. For example, in Lower East Side (New York City) '[t]he artists were

13   See the homonymous brochure, Katrin Fischer et al. *Revitalisation through arts and culture: new
     developments for 5 European industrial complexes*. Nürnberg: Second Chance (2012) http://www.
     secondchanceproject.eu/wp/wp-content/uploads/2012/11/SECOND-CHANCE_Mid-Project-
     Brochure_online_final.pdf, reviewed 1 October, 2013.

14   Matteo Pasquinelli, 'Beyond the Ruins of the Creative City: Berlin's Factory of Culture and the
     Sabotage of Rent,' KUNSTrePUBLIK (eds), *Skulpturenpark Berlin_Zentrum*. Berlin: Verlag der
     Buchhandlung Walther König (2010)

15   David Harvey, 'The Art of Rent: Globalisation, Monopoly and the Commodification of Culture'
     (2001). http://www.generation-online.org/c/fc_rent1.htm

16   Matteo Pasquinelli, 'Beyond the Ruins of the Creative City: Berlin's Factory of Culture and the
     Sabotage of Rent,' KUNSTrePUBLIK (eds.): *Skulpturenpark Berlin_Zentrum*. Berlin: Verlag der
     Buchhandlung Walther König (2010).

17   David Harvey, 'The Right to the City.' *New Left Review* 53 (September-October 2008): 31.

18   Sharon Zukin, *The Cultures of Cities*, Cambridge: Blackwell, 1995, p. 111.

pioneers of gentrification in this new frontier for the middle class, by creating an art scene and community, combining the use of their space for living, producing, performing and exhibiting.'[19]

Instead of what Zukin[20] termed 'artistic mode of production', the parasitism through which the *Second Chance* has been building upon its campaign, is availing to the emplaced and sediment collective symbolic capital. It also accumulated during the socialistic industrial era and strongly underlined the embedded collective memory. The 'unique cultural assets'[21] of the former Rog industrial complex are in fact just '[...] special marks of distinction that attach to some place, as they have a significant drawing power upon the flows of capital more generally.'[22] Concisely, claims to the uniqueness yield monopoly rent.[23]

I shall underline here another passage from the project's description: 'The cities face the same challenges of *developing a heritage and landmarked former industrial sites*'.[24] The claim indicates that the accumulation of the *collective symbolic capital* would combine a symbolic musealization of the localized 'unique' socialist remains *with* the outlined cultural capital (the projected art spaces and institutions) *in order to*, lastly, pave the way for capital accumulation under the banner of creative industries. Thus, the traditional way of gentrification will intertwine the (pseudo)modern and the artificial form.

One of the premises of the pan-European *Second Chance* is therefore purely teleological: the cognitariat would superimpose the bygone proletariat which once laboured in these spaces spanning from shipbuilders to bicycle factory workers. What is a better way to illuminate the triumph of the bright 'progressive' capitalism over the obscure 'archaic' socialism? Here also could fit the statement of the MOL's Head of Department for Culture expressed at the unveiling of the new plans (which will be discussed in more detail later). According to her, Rog will become a point of interest for the new generation

---

19   Anonymous. *The Occupation of art and gentrification* (1989) pp.7. http://theanarchistlibrary.org/ library/anonymous-the-occupation-of-art-and-gentrification#fn_back7

20   Sharon Zukin, *Loft Living: Culture and Capital in Urban Change*, Baltimore and London: The Johns Hopkins University Press, 1982.

21   The phrase is taken from the announcement of the public presentation carried out by Lia Ghilardi in the City Museum at MOL's invitation (see Second Chance 2012).

22   David Harvey, 'The Art of Rent: Globalisation, Monopoly and the Commodification of Culture' (2001). http://www.generation-online.org/c/fc_rent1.htm

23   Ibid.

24   Second Chance, *Project Description* (2013) Emphasis mine. http://www.secondchanceproject.eu/ wp/?page_id=26.

of young architects and designers, which will 'get in the city centre a space and tools for entering the labor market'.[25]

Moreover, by perpetually referring to the *disused* and *(former) Rog factory* the *Second Chance* is not only imaginarily discarding the emplaced collective body from the past of a Yugoslav industrial flagship, but rather the recuperation is broadened onto the semantic level with a metonymy, castling the factory's original denomination (i.e. Rog) and by continuously repeating the Rog's (distorted) condition. The capitalist exploitation coated itself in 'creativity' abandoning the division between former/present, as the case of Rog shows. The denial of this binarity is necessary, or else the legitimacy of subjectivities present within Rog would be acknowledged.

In this view, an left-out part of the *Second Chance* description is to be understood: '[These postindustrial sites are] the industrial estates who deserve this 2nd chance.'[26] The positioning of the *Second Chance* in the linear continuation of the paternalistic logic of urbanism (the anthropomorphized discourse of giving estates a second opportunity)[27] is actively denying the collective reappropiation of the space in 2006 as well as it is denying the ongoing manifold autonomous cultural, social, and political production being housed in the buildings.[28] This attempt to revive a space already revived[29] can signal only one thing: creative industries will lie on the ashes of autonomous collective creativity. One could go that far to delineate the latter as a fetishist urban necrophilia: the compulsive reuse of the moribund object-factory as a stimulus of capital consolation (or better yet, accumulation). It is an object to which either any of the current vivacity is apathetically negated, either to which the emancipating collective creativity will be institutionally euthanized by turning it into an urban corpse—or only to be repossessed later. Once the collective creative capital failed to undergo capitalist valorization, the only attraction left to the capital and managerial establishment is to cling to the cadaveric proletarian collective 'body'.

---

25 Demšič in Krajčinović. Nina Krajčinović, 'Rog kot politični projekt brez zagotovljenih sredstev', *Delo* 5th September 2013, http://www.delo.si/novice/ljubljana/rog-kot-politicni-projekt-brez-zagotovljenih-sredstev.html

26 Second Chance, *Project Description* (2013). http://www.secondchanceproject.eu/wp/?page_id=26.

27 A topic deserving its own Foucauldian analysis is not just the inflation of euphemisms for gentrification but also the medical, anthropomorphized, and biopolitical urbanistic discourses (e.g. revitalisation, regeneration, reanimation, rehabilitation, sustainable, degraded, sanitation).

28 Initially the entire multitude in Rog was nonchalantly ignored from any description whatsoever. However, the current and updated version of the project's website is recognizing the contemporary murmurings in the Rog's building—altogether in one sentence: "Since 2006 the building is being used on a daily basis by temporary users who developed cultural, artistic, sport and social activities on site" (Second Chance 2013).

29 Nenad Jelesijević, Rog med razlastitvijo in prilastitvijo skupnega. Radio Študent (5 April 2012). http://radiostudent.si/kultura/dlako-z-jezika/rog-med-razlastitvijo-in-prilastitvijo-skupnega

Pointed out by Pasquinelli, Harvey's *collective symbolic capital* can be conceived as another name for the '*capitalist exploitation of the commons*—a form of exploitation that does not need violent enclosures'.[30] Here the notion of violence deserves further attention. Ever since Rog's reappropriation, MOL is intentionally leaving Rog in deficient circumstances, without the minimal material conditions; ever since the reappropriation the whole complex is functioning in abstraction of electricity.[31] Rog's users are quotidianly experiencing systematic exhaustion, longitudinal vegetation on their bodies, and, generally, the menace of eviction—all instances of subtle structural violence strongly calling into question the presumed no-violence-policy of capital exploitation.

Now I can focus on the postulation regarding the *exploitation of the commons*. We are faced with the notion of the exploited commons, which is easily applicable to the enunciated capitalistic mode of production as immaterial, pertaining to cognitive, affective labour. This appears be the position after the implementation of *Second Chance*, turning Rog from a closedown factory into an immaterial social factory. Again, according to the description the project's intention is: '[...] to transform a disused industrial site in a *cultural and creative work and living space* [...]'.[32] The phrase quintessentially comprises the concept of bio-political production, in which all spheres of social life are produced: '[...] post-Fordism and the immaterial paradigm of production adopt performativity, communication, and collaboration as central characteristics'.[33] Perhaps this is an opportune time to fasten more particularly the pervasive creation of the creative industries.

In the White Cube, a Simulacrum of the Creative Industries: RogLab Centre Pilot Project

The capital's colonization of the public spaces and the commons once was exemplified in 2012 with the so called RogLab Centre Pilot Project. Installed as a plot investment of the *Second Chance* project and located on the embankment directly across the street from Rog, RogLab takes a shape of an entirely white cargo container. Here we have a double interpretation of an object pioneering the local creative industries, offering itself. The white container cannot be seen only as the advocate of the White Cube and thus

---

30 Matteo Pasquinelli, 'Beyond the Ruins of the Creative City: Berlin's Factory of Culture and the Sabotage of Rent,' KUNSTrePUBLIK (eds): *Skulpturenpark Berlin_Zentrum*. Berlin: Verlag der Buchhandlung Walther König (2010)

31 This situation is somewhat being compensated by relying on the usage of electricity generators that require an increasingly larger amount of money for each organized event.

32 Second Chance, *Project Description* (2013). Emphasis mine. http://www.secondchanceproject.eu/wp/?page_id=26

33 Michael Hardt and Antonio Negri, *Multitude: War and Democracy in the Age of Empire*, New York: Penguin Press, 2004, p. 200.

flagging the penetration of the new 'creative' urban economy; the container is simultaneously a prime example of a boxed up neoliberalism through which the mantra of
free movements of goods, capital, services and people, is transmitted around the globe.
By analogy with Giddens' the conceptualization of the state as a territorial (bordered)
power-container, RogLab strains in presenting itself as an unconfined 'creative' power
container and a dynamo for the creative economy:

> RogLab is conceived as a production, educational and presentation space in a 30
> m^2-container object. It is dedicated to activities in the fields of architecture, design
> and contemporary art, their mutual connecting and cross-sector collaboration (econ-
> omy, education, science, environment, space...) as well as international networking.[34]

RogLab's spatial separation from the Rog building by being *outside* yet *in face of* it, does
not mean its contents are hermetically encapsulated or, at first glance, antithetic to those
nourished in Rog.[35] Quite to the contrary: this act of colonization of the public space
means as well the colonization of creativity by being the epistemological and material
forerunner of the creative industries in the area. For example, RogLab is openly acknowl-
edging the devastation of Rog; it promotes to be 'an attractive mobile architecture [...]
marking the beginning of the renovation of the former Rog factory. The pilot project will
function as a small scale model of the future Rog Centre'.[36]

Further, on the external surface of RogLab an imprinted characterization reads: 'In the
3D workshop for fast prototyping, we help you *develop ideas into tangible products*.'[37]
Thus, the neoliberal capitalist paradigm of productive knowledge is canalized into an
applicable and vendible market form. 'Neoliberalism,' asserts Harvey[38] '[...] proposes
that human well-being can best be advanced by liberating individual entrepreneurial
freedoms and skills within an institutional framework characterized by strong private
property rights, free markets, and free trade. The role of the state is to create and preserve an institutional framework appropriate to such practices.'

Taken together, Rog*Lab* can indeed be viewed as *labor*-atorial, a laboratorial materializa-
tion reflecting the intertwined processes of the capitalist rent parasiting on the produc-

---

34   Rog Centre Pilot Project, *About* (2013) http://www.roglab.si/en/about

35   This separation is also an uncanny physical evidence of not accepting the present situation of the
     living self-organized communities in Rog.

36   Second Chance, Rog Centre of Contemporary Arts (2013), http://www.secondchanceproject.eu/
     wp/?page_id=94

37   Ibid. Emphasis mine.

38   David Harvey, *A Brief History of Neoliberalism*, Oxford: Oxford University Press, 2005, p.2.

tive commons,[39] incorporation of existent subversion, commodification of autonomous collective creativity, and the (forerunner and justifier of) spatial usurpation.[40] The paradigmatic workshop/art project 'Socialdress' carried out in RogLab might be the utmost illustration of these processes *in vitro*. Championing the creative industries, the workshop sucked out the labour of unemployed women who were voluntarily embroidering clothes for several days:

> This art project [...] takes place in the form of a clothes and household fabrics fashion collection. The collection incorporates slogans from the recent Slovenian protests[41]—the expression of the general public's rebellion and dissatisfaction with the existing system. Modern embroidery machines will be used to embroider the selected slogans onto fabrics and clothes, thus empowering them. Traditional craft skills, modern technology, fashion, social engagement, activism and social entrepreneurship all join forces in this new interdisciplinary art project [...].[42]

The machine of commodification, which mimics under the coat of benevolence and social responsibility, attempted to decontextualize and castrate the collective subversive potentiality of the uprisings by aestheticization and banalization, vampirizing the free labour: 'The [Socialdress] project promotes and supports sewing e.g. dress home-making. It transforms the sewing into an entertaining and useful social activity'.[43] Here, the unpaid social cooperation, the mutual production, and interdisciplinary collaboration all go a step further from the individualism inherent to the anatomized precariat. The neoliberal machine does not base its agenda anymore on explicit exclusion, but rather on the controlled inclusion—preferably the collective one. In this vein, it is necessary to mention the emphasis of the *Second Chance* on the newly incarnated neoliberal species, who do not go under the name stockholders or shareholders but stakeholders instead. According to Marx's general intellect or to Kropotkin's mutual aid, a neoliberal counterpart is allocated and linked with the fabrication of consent through a Habermassian ideal

---

39   Carlo Vercellone, *The New Articulation of Wages, Rent and Profit in Cognitive Capitalism* (2008). http://halshs.archives-ouvertes.fr/docs/00/26/55/84/PDF/The_new_ articulation_of_wagesHall1. pdf

40   Such intents were already detectable during the proposal to erect the Centre of Contemporary Arts.

41   To give few examples of protest slogans coined by the popular anger to be later embroidered: "*gotof si*" (you are finished!), "*fertik je*" (it's over), "*vse jih bomo nesli vun*" (we'll take them all out), "*ulice so naše*" (the streets are ours), "*lopovi!*" (crooks!), "*moč ljudem, ne strankam*" (power to the people, not to parties).

42   Rog Centre Pilot Project. *Socialdress—Power to the People* (2013), http://www.roglab.si/en/ fresh/2013/socialdress_empowering_people

43   Marija Mojca Pungerčar, ND (2013), http://www.3via.org/index.php?htm=mojca

communication and rational discourse. Throughout the practice of the *Second Chance*, the colonization of the commons goes hand in hand with the adoption of the formalized 'inclusive bottom-up participatory' smokescreen.

Gentrification Goes Public

What was to be witnessed in 2013 was another twist in the neoliberal municipal urban policies. In the explication of the changed spatial plan for Rog, under the heading '*Assessment of the situation, causes and aims why the document is necessary*' the scenario runs: since the initial blueprint was approved, the situation, especially economic, has been changing and the arrangement of Rog's area to the extent of the previous spatial plan was no longer possible. In reality, no private investor was willing to take part in the *Second Chance*, thereby decelerating the entire process of the execution; indeed, an irony derived directly out of the global financial crisis. Neither the downfall of a private-public partnership or the subsequent resignation of capital did not bury the peculiar spatial voracity. Notwithstanding the financial deficit and the public debt, the construction pretence is now to be orchestrated by the municipality independently of the investments from the private sector.

Therefore, a changed spatial plan was proposed enabling the construction in several stages. More accurately, a seven-phased (re)construction is now being designed. In the first stage of the construction, the blueprint includes two crucial interventions: the 'outside arrangement' around the central building *and* an underground garage overlapping with the position of almost all buildings on the territory of Rog.[44] In all likelihood, the planned besiegement of the central building and the 'outside arrangement' will manifest itself directly in the form of an internal reconstruction of the main factory outbuilding, leaving behind another 'late capitalist hollow space'.[45]

As for the surrounding buildings without the historical preservation,[46] which itself allows façadism—and the demolition of the building's interior yet leaving its exterior intact—these will be levelled to the ground, causing another symptomatic fenced urban void, filled at the best with gravelled parking spaces, as this profitable emptiness is the *modus operandi* for architectural shortfalls in the city. What would evidently distinguish it from other urban voids caused by the lack of investments is contained in the intention of transforming the building into a politically silent urban phantom. The

---

44   MOL 2013.

45   Ernst Bloch, 'Building in Empty Spaces', in Bloch, Ernst: *The Utopian Function of Art and Literature* Cambridge, Massachusetts: MIT Press (1959/1996): 185-198.

46   The urbanistic taxidermy sparing the main factory outbuilding will be performed because it falls under the cultural heritage protection (cf. The Institute for the Protection of Cultural Heritage of Slovenia 2008, 45).

eviction of users, the fencing off potential occupants, and seclusion are all practical strategies of de-politization. In other words, the complete resignation from the project remains unimaginable since gentrification operates in a broader urban context. With the restructuration into a 'postindustrial creative site' though, the refashioned Rog factory will, at best, become the situated gravitational field for gentrification, as the process of gentrification will inevitably include the entire surrounding neighbourhood.

'Gentrification is class war'

The fundamental reason behind the repeatedly converted plans of demolishment of the liberated Rog factory area seems simple;[47] communities 'that swarm in Rog, are not dangerous for MOL because of the revitalization of [...] abandoned spaces, but because of the swarming of new and different forms of social activities, connections and collaboration'.[48] The eradication and neutralization, discursive or violently material, of autonomous collective creativity, troubling the flows of capital, are inevitably inherent to wider processes of capital accumulation. For once, in the current condition, the extraction of monopoly rent as the business model in cognitive capitalism (Pasquinelli 2010) is obstructed. In the hegemonic notion of the collective creativity, we run into the creativity as ideological substitution for labour. The creativity as understood by the apologist of corporative creative industries has not become the Deleuzian becoming, but an ideological superstructure of labour and therefore exploitation.

Beuys' famous claim fulfils itself in an odd manner—in the age of cognitive capitalism, elevating each and every individual into divinity, everyone is not an artist, but a *creator*. Fortunately, the repolitization of creativity and its emancipation from the neoliberal colonial deadlock are being collectively produced in factories of the Foucauldian insurrectional subjugated knowledge. The remaining question is whether one will hop on the moving train rushing through the urbanscape moved by these machines.

References

Anonymous. 1989. *The Occupation of art and gentrification.* Internet source: http://theanarchis-tlibrary.org/library/anonymous-the-occupation-of-art-and-gentrification#fn_back7, reviewed October 1, 2013.

Bloch, Ernst. 'Building in Empty Spaces,' in Bloch, Ernst: *The Utopian Function of Art and Litera-ture.* Cambridge, Massachusetts: MIT Press, 1959/1996, pp. 185-198.

Bourdieu, Pierre and Loïc Wacquant. 'NewLiberalSpeak. Notes on the new planetary vulgate.'

---

47   The urban plans of MOL can be, to some extent, seen as the tactic response to the claims during the temporal occupation: the problem of empty premises, the lack of a clear strategy with Rog, the need of spaces for sociocultural production etc.

48   Marta Gregorčič, 'Rog—presenečanja, iz katerih rojijo multitude.' *Časopis za kritiko znanosti,* 34 / 223 (2006): 7-10.

Radical Philosophy 105 (2001) pp. 1-5.

Florida, Richard. *Cities and the Creative Class.* London, New York: Routledge, 2005.

Gregorčič, Marta. 'Rog—presenečanja, iz katerih rojijo multitude.' *Časopis za kritiko znanosti,* 34 -223 (2006) pp. 7-10.

Hardt, Michael and Antonio Negri. *Multitude: War and Democracy in the Age of Empire.* New York: Penguin Press, 2004.

Harvey, David. 'The Art of Rent: Globalisation, Monopoly and the Commodification of Culture' (2001). http://www.generation-online.org/c/fc_rent1.htm

Harvey, David. *A Brief History of Neoliberalism.* Oxford: Oxford University Press, 2005.

Harvey, David. 'The Right to the City.' *New Left Review,* 53 Sept. Oct (2008): 23-40.

Institute for Civilisation and Culture. *SWOT Analysis for the Purposes of the Revitalisation of the Former Rog Factory with the Establishment of the Rog—Centre of Contemporary Arts.* (2011) Internet source: http://www.secondchanceproject.eu/wp/wp-content/uploads/2011/07/SWOT_Analysis_Ljubljana.pdf

Jelesijević, Nenad. Rog med razlastitvijo in prilastitvijo skupnega. Radio Študent (5 April 2012). Internet source: http://radiostudent.si/kultura/dlako-z-jezika/rog-med-razlastitvijo-in-prilastit-vijo-skupnega

Krajčinović, Nina. Rog kot politični projekt brez zagotovljenih sredstev. *Delo* (5 September 2013) http://www.delo.si/novice/ljubljana/rog-kot-politicni-projekt-brez-zagotovljenih-sredstev.html

Katrin Fischer et al. *Revitalisation through arts and culture: new developments for 5 European industrial complexes.* Nürnberg: Second Chance (2012) http://www.secondchanceproject.eu/wp/wp-content/uploads/2012/11/SECOND-CHANCE_Mid-Project-Brochure_online_final.pdf>, reviewed 1 October, 2013.

Kurnik, Andrej and Barbara Beznec. 'Resident Alien: The Rog Experience on the Margin,' in Radical Education Collective (eds) *New public spaces: dissensual political and artistic practices in the post-Yugoslav context.* Maastricht: Jan van Eyck Academie, 2009, pp. 45-62. http://radical.temp.si/reader/AndrejBarbara.pdf

Kurnik, Andrej. *Vzamimo si mesto!* (2013), http://www.njetwork.org/Vzamimo-si-mesto

Landry, Charles. *The Creative City: A Toolkit for Urban Innovators.* London: Earthscan, 2000.

Mihelič, Breda et al. *Les anciennes usines 'Rog'/Ljubljana : exemple Européen de mise en valeur du patrimoine architectural abandonné : actes du 4ème Colloque Eurocultures, Ljubljana: 29 mai—2 juin* (1995), Brussels: Institut Supérieur d'Architecture Saint-Luc.

MOL. 2013. *Dopolnjeni osnutek Odloka o spremembah in dopolnitvah Odloka o občinskem podrobnem prostorskem načrtu za del območja urejanja CI 5/6 Rog,* http://www.ljubljana.si/file/1351552/dop_osn_spr_oppn_ci56.pdf

Pasquinelli, Matteo. 'Beyond the Ruins of the Creative City: Berlin's Factory of Culture and the Sabotage of Rent', in KUNSTrePUBLIK (eds), *Skulpturenpark Berlin_Zentrum.* Berlin: Verlag der Buchhandlung Walther König, 2010.

Pungerčar, Marija Mojca. ND, http://www.3via.org/index.php?htm=mojca

Rog Centre Pilot Project. *About,* (2013) http://www.roglab.si/en/about

Rog Centre Pilot Project. *Socialdress—Power to the People* (2013), http://www.roglab.si/en/fresh/2013/socialdress_empowering_people

Sassen, Saskia. 'Locating cities on global circuits.' *Environment & Urbanization* 14 (2002): 13-30.

http://www.rrojasdatabank.info/urban/euv14n1p13.pdf

Second Chance. *Project Description* (2013). Internet source: http://www.secondchanceproject.eu/wp/?page_id=26

Second Chance. The Former Rog Factory (2013) Internet source: http://www.secondchanceproject.eu/wp/?page_id=16

Second Chance. Rog Centre of Contemporary Arts (2013). Internet source: http://www.secondchanceproject.eu/wp/?page_id=94

Second Chance. Can Culture Alone Regenerate Places? (2012), http://www.secondchanceproject.eu/wp/?p=1112

TEMP. 'TEMP about TEMP, or a quick and unsystematic retrospective of the workings of one temporary and informal multidisciplinary group.' In: Radical Education Collective (eds.): *New public spaces: dissensual political and artistic practices in the post-Yugoslav context.* Maastricht: Jan van Eyck Academie (2009): 144-158, http://radical.temp.si/reader/TEMP.pdf

The Institute for the Protection of Cultural Heritage of Slovenia *STROKOVNE ZASNOVE VARSTVA KULTURNE DEDIŠČINE za območje MESTNE OBČINE LJUBLJANA* (2008), http://giskd2s.situla.org/evrdd/SZ/eVRD_SZ_Ljubljana_2008_02_00.pdf

Vercellone, Carlo. *The New Articulation of Wages, Rent and Profit in Cognitive Capitalism* (2008)., http://halshs.archives-ouvertes.fr/docs/00/26/55/84/PDF/The_new_ articulation_of_wagesHall1.pdf

Zukin, Sharon. *Loft Living: Culture and Capital in Urban Change,* Baltimore and London: The Johns Hopkins University Press, 1982.

Zukin, Sharon. *Landscapes of Power: From Detroit to Disney World,* Berkeley: University of California Press, 1991.

Zukin, Sharon. *The Cultures of Cities,* Cambridge: Blackwell, 1995.

NEOLIBERALISM AND THE AUTONOMY OF ART: THE CULTURE OF POWER, THE POWER OF CULTURE[1]

IRMGARD EMMELHEINZ

In Mexico, advanced neoliberal reforms are taking place at a much faster pace than in other parts of the world. These reforms have not only delivered new forms of life and making a living, but also created new sensibilities. The erosion of the social contract brought on by these reforms, has had tangible, negative effects on the social tissue. This has materialized, for example, in what is known as the most violent and dangerous city in the world, Ciudad Juárez, where in 2010 alone 3000 people were killed. Bearing this in mind, I define neoliberalism as a *sensibility* that shapes subjectivities, permeates art and culture, differentiates and homogenizes people, molds lives and desires, mistakes information for knowledge, gives shape to space and thus to social relations, normalizes violence, creates ways of seeing the world that justify destruction and dispossession with notions progress and development, or that tries to solve economic precarity through self-help and permanent education. I argue that neoliberalism is more than a system that is ruled by a free market economy, which implies the privatization of the welfare state and an array of government services (for example: education, health, energy), subcontracting to the private sector and changes in labor laws and worker's rights as well as a transnational division of labor. The system of control under neoliberalism combines a militarized police regime with repressive tolerance, the logic of securitization with granting freedom of expression and 'quality of life'. The political figures, molded and governed by the neoliberal regime itself are: the *homo oeconomicus* (the entrepreneur responsible for his own well-being and manager of his own human capital) and the subject of rights (the State is in charge of guaranteeing that his human rights are respected). Aside from an economic-political system, I see neoliberalism as a way of relating to the world, to nature, to things and beings, which presupposes unlimited growth and development. It is also a way of living and working: human beings are put to work beyond their capacities, erasing the distinction between leisure and work time. Neoliberalism is also a sensibility that establishes the terms of empathy and sympathy and has outlined a new notion of alterity. Configured as 'social responsibility' or social work, to 'help' the Other means to focus on the (so-called) 'secondary malfunctions' of the current capitalist system by disseminating personal and managerial practices such as tolerance, showing respect, nurturing dialogue, transparency and social collaboration. In this sense, the 'Other' is a 'community to come', the 'subject of rights' (to ethical restitution: refugees, displaced, immigrants, those who live under a 'state of exception'), the *underclass*, that is, he or she

---

1   Different versions of this essay were presented at Bureau Publik, Copenhagen, 31 October 2013 and KHIB in Bergen, Norway, on 5 November 2013.

who will be permanently outside globalizing processes, including access to education, jobs and consumption. The category of the 'Other' encompasses political and religious fundamentalists as well: fanatics who are outside globalizing and modernizing processes by choice. These *Others* are sometimes given faces in the media or in art by spectacular-izing their subjectivity but obviating the processes that render their lives precarious and endangered in the first place.

What has this got to do with the autonomy of art? As we will see, postmodernism put art and culture at the center of social, political and economic processes. They are now inex-tricable from work, production, consumption and subjectivity: in the neoliberal regime, art in particular and culture in general are used actively as compensation and improve-ment of tools, all the while normalizing and spreading the antithesis of autonomous art, that is, 'useful art'. Subsumed to political action, much of contemporary art has taken up a political role as either 'sensible politics' or 'socially engaged artwork'. This is tied to the fact that in our current world order, as Marina Vishmidt and Kerstin Stakemeier point out, 'art no longer designates a reproductive and representational realm, but one of productivity and social power' and thus the autonomy of art itself has become a prob-lem—in so far as it has become a realm for the production of added value.[2]

In the September 2013 editorial of *e-flux journal,* editors Juliete Aranda, Brian Kuan Wood and Anton Vidokle stated that art is produced at a double bind: while art can be complicit in or instrumentalized by power, its autonomy is located in an imaginary space. What do they mean by this? First, that art, in order to be *seen,* depends on a platform—an institution—and thus needs to be part of some art world. Second, that the autonomy of art—as a separate regime or an isolated sphere—is a fantasy. In order to consider the autonomy of art outside of this double bind, Clement Greenberg tied the autonomy of art—as art's for art's sake—to the avant-garde situating criticality within the discipline or medium of art itself. In Greenberg's definition, avant-garde (modernist) painting clearly takes a position against socialist realist painting and those debates of the 1930s that rely on the relationship between art and politics (embodied for example by Mexican muralist painting, which was very popular in New York in the 1930s). He characterizes avant-garde by its self-critique in the sense that its formal expression is a meditation on the qualities of the medium of painting. This meant extricating figuration from the arts, and an essentialist understanding of the mediums of art: for Greenberg, 'purity' was political—especially if it was seen as an embodiment of a free nation versus the authoritarian Soviet Union.

Postmodernism could be understood as an effort to break with Greenberg's disciplinary totalitarianism. Taking up the Dadaist and surrealist avant-garde's goals of unifying art

---

2   Kerstin Stakemeier and Marina Vishmidt, 'The Value of Autonomy: A conversation between Kerstin
      Stakemeier and Marina Vishmidt about the reproduction of art,' *Texte zur Kunst* 88 (December
      2012): 102-117.

and life, postmodernism thrived on the advent of interdisciplinary strategies and the symbiosis of art with everything else. Post-war art continued the vanguardist critique of the bourgeois notions of autonomous art and expressive artists. It embraced everyday objects, transformed the artist's function, questioned the institution of art and attacked it in an anarchist manner.[3] Following Hal Foster, art from the 1950s and 1960s represents the failure to destroy the institution of art and the institutionalization of the avant-garde.[4] If Greenberg advocated aesthetic autonomy with the purpose of resisting the illustrational meanings typical of kitsch and commercial forces, post-modernist's interdisciplinary strategies led art, in Foster's words, 'to become embedded into life under the terms of mass capitalism, while it became appropriated by the culture industry'.[5] Due to its 'post-medium' condition, as Rosalind Krauss termed 'postmodern interdisciplinarity', art is enmeshed with reality, and its materials can range from and beyond social interaction to scientific research and montage. With postmodernism, the politics of the autonomy of art meant breaking away from in Greenberg's sense of purity and thus art's autonomy came to be conceived as 'provisional, always defined diacritically (as something supplemental to art) and situated politically, always *semi*'.[6]

Beyond postmodernism, parallel to an increase of corporate subsidies to the arts, there has been a recent boom in private collecting and thus a market boom. The value of art is speculative and reflects the logic of finance-based economy (and risk): the economy and critical art share the core value of 'innovation'. In this regard, neoliberalism has meant privatization for the arts or the collusion between the private and the public sector in order to subsidize them. In the past decade or so (and in the US long before that), corporations have played an important role in investing in culture. Institutions and corporations have been seeking to play an important role in communicating the point of view of the private sector on an array of critical public topics.[7] If art was previously supported by the state, because culture was considered to be an asset to the nation, today, corporations have appropriated this function, as they sponsor and jury art shows, grant awards and funds and collect artworks. Meanwhile, they promote their perspectives on critical public topics.[8] In a 1998 article, art historian Chin-tao Wu highlighted how corporations appropriate the concept of innovation—also known as innovative disruption

---

3   Hal Foster, 'What's Neo about the Neo-Avant-Garde?' *October*, Vol. 70, The Duchamp Effect (Autumn 1994): 5-32.

4   Foster, 'What's Neo about the Neo-Avant-Garde?'.

5   Foster, 'What's Neo about the Neo-Avant-Garde?'.

6   Foster, 'What's Neo about the Neo-Avant-Garde?'.

7   Gregory Sholette, 'Welcome to the Desert of the Real Artworld,' *Oxford Art Journal* 27.2, (2004), p. 259. http://www.gregorysholette.com/wp-content/uploads/2011/04/07_welcome1.pdf.

8   Sholette, 'Welcome to the Desert of the Real Artworld,' pp. 260-261.

or creative destruction—in order to redefine its meaning in corporate terms. She quotes John Murphy, executive vice-president of Philip Morris Inc—a U.S. cigarette company—on their sponsorship of the 1969 exhibition, *When Attitudes Become Form*:

> We feel it is appropriate that we participate in bringing these works to the attention of the public, for there is a key element in this 'new art' which has its counterpart in the business world. That element is innovation—without which it would be impossible for progress to be made in any segment in society.[9]

Furthermore, in the context of neoliberal reforms and sensibilities, there is a global tendency to subdue contemporary art to the politics of culture administration, which implies 'democratizing culture' making it accessible to the masses, using it as a tool for the well-being of society, and the reconstruction or healing of a community or society that has experienced violence. Cultural institutions subsidized by corporations and individual patrons apparently follow progressive agendas promoting political or socially minded art. For instance, *Creative Time* in New York (funded by a mix of state and corporate support) supports public and community art, with the goal of enabling the politicization of social space with cultural intervention. This organization sponsored Tania Bruguera's *Immigrant Movement International*, a project developed in Queens, New York in 2011, which the artist describes as: a flexible community space and long-term socio-political movement, public workshops, events, actions and partnerships with immigrant and service organizations. The artist further qualified her project as 'useful art'.[10] The problem is that initiatives such as this one, render opaque the real economic conditions that led to situations of immigrant precarity to begin with; immigrants are local signs of complex global forces operating on conditions of life and work at home and abroad. Many would argue that to subsidize a project like Bruguera's signals the transfer of social work to artistic work funded by the private sector. Politics comes into the scene through art as social work in the name of 'public interest', only to become subject to administration, engineering and a technocratic way of administering social problems, configuring the private version of the welfare state.[11] Furthermore, as corporate support to the establishment of antagonistic spaces becomes gradually institutionalized within society, the question rises, after Gregory Sholette, 'Who owns cultural capital and who has the right to use it?' For him, corporate involvement in the arts is akin, or perhaps integral, to the current erosion of public space.[12] Moreover, as cultural spaces become institutional

9   Chin-Tao Wu, 'Embracing the Enterprise Culture: Art Institutions Since the 1980s', *New Left Review* I/230, (July-August 1998): 31.

10   See artist's statement available at: http://www.taniabruguera.com/cms/486-0-Immigrant+Movement+International.htm.

11   Oliver Marchart, 'Art, Space and the Public Sphere(s)', 2002, http://eipcp.net/transversal/0102/marchart/en.

12   Sholette, 'Welcome to the Desert of the Real Artworld'.

bastions of democratic self-expression and sites for social reconciliation and self-help, dissent is criminalized and forcefully punished worldwide.

It becomes evident that art and culture are central to neoliberal processes that act as agents of globalization and as tools for improvement and development, counterinsurgency and pacification. An extreme example of this could be the 'culturally sensible' occupation of Iraq as described by Nato Thompson (director of *Creative Time*). In uncritical terms, Thompson recounts how General David Petraeus wrote a field manual geared at changing people's attitudes towards the American occupation of Mosul:

> [It is] a story about counterinsurgency and community organizing, about getting to know people as an occupying force, and getting to know people as neighbors. It is a story about the military entering the terrain of that thing called culture.[13]

In this regard, a 'cultural approach' to military occupation is akin to artistic social and community practices, as both involve 'getting to know people to be able to change the landscapes of life and of power'.[14] In the case of civilians in Mosul, this is done by obviating their experiences of being under attack. This cultural turn in the U.S. military machinery took place a few years after theorist Frederic Jameson diagnosed a 'cultural turn' in capitalism, arguing that social space had been completely saturated with the image of culture. This is because in professional and daily activities, as well as in the various forms of entertainment we enjoy, society consumes cultural products all the time. The postmodern 'cultural turn' diagnosed by Jameson, was further elaborated by George Yúdice upon observing (in 2003) that the uses of culture had undergone an unprecedented expansion not just in the marketplace but also along social, political, and economic lines. According to Yúdice, since the state and corporations already utilize culture as a tool as they search for economic and sociopolitical betterment, culture has become a resource and a compensatory device to the ravages neoliberal policies have caused on social tissue: both give meaning and symbolic representations, provide mechanisms of solace, as well as function as tools for re-invention and amelioration.[15] In this context, the line between public programs and relational aesthetics or participative

13   Nato Thompson, 'The Insurgents Part I: Community-Based Practice as Military Methodology,' *e-flux journal* # 47, (September 2013), http://www.e-flux.com/journal/the-insurgents-part-i-community-based-practice-as-military-methodology. In the second part of his essay, Thompson includes a disclaimer about him glossing over U.S. military violence in Iraq. See: http://www.e-flux.com/journal/the-insurgents-part-ii-fighting-the-left-by-being-the-left.

14   Thompson, 'The Insurgents Part I'.

15   See Irmgard Emmelhainz, 'Art and the Cultural Turn: Farewell to Committed Autonomous Art?', *e-flux journal* N. 42 (February 2013), http://www.e-flux.com/journal/art-and-the-cultural-turn-farewell-to-committed-autonomous-art.

art appears to be increasingly blurred. Former Mexican president Felipe Calderón made a public appearance in February 2012 in Ciudad Juárez in front of a sign that read: 'No More Weapons'. The billboard measured 8×21 meters, and was built by soldiers of the National Defense Department with 3 tons of assault weapons that were confiscated at the Mexican border and molten into bricks. During the ceremony in which the billboard was unveiled, Calderón turned toward the Mexican-American border and begged the U.S. (in bad English): 'No more weapons! Dear friends of the United States, Mexico needs your help to stop this terrible violence we are suffering'. During this trip, Calderón also participated in the destruction of 6 thousand confiscated weapons, and planted a tree at a Community Center. Calderon's propagandistic gestures immediately recall the language of socially engaged contemporary art, particularly, Pedro Reyes' intervention, *Palas por Pistolas* in Culiacán in 2008 (also executed in Juárez in the same week of Calderon's visit). Reyes' project of exchanging shovels for weapons was subsidized by two pre-dominant Mexican corporations: Trupper, which produces hardware, and Coppel, which sells appliances and other goods. For this project, Reyes devised a Television campaign inviting citizens to give up their weapons in exchange for a coupon for appliances. The artist collected 1527 weapons, which were destroyed at a military zone in a public act. Giving his action a further twist, Reyes sought to have the rests of the weapons welded together to produce 1527 shovels carrying an inscription telling the story of the weapon they represented (this was not possible due to technical reasons, so Trupper ended up donating them). The engraved shovels were distributed in art institutions and public schools. Adults and children planted 1527 trees. To Reyes, this ritual had a pedagogical purpose: 'to show the people how an agent of death can become an agent of life'.[16] A similar public purge of weapons in exchange for appliances (and tablets), is currently happening in Mexico City led by a 'Pink Ladies Brigade'. These relational actions—both by General Petraeus' and by the Mexican government—show how the language of contemporary art has been appropriated by propaganda for its purposes, making politics and aesthetics indistinguishable, as both operate in the realm of symbolic and perceptive work. These are also examples of the predominant idea that violence can be eased—or appeased—through cultural intervention and in the Mexican case, by giving away highly desirable goods.

Aside from this 'artistic approach' to social, political and military action, sensible production has taken up a political function. Political work has been developed into a matter of codification using medial forms with the purpose of creating a terrain for political acts, creating an 'activist imaginary' made of political fields constituted by images. Political action embedded in cultural forms implies making things public as a way of signs.[17] An

---

16   Artist's statement available online: http://pedroreyes.net/palasporpistolas.php(http://newleftreview.org/I/87-88/theodor-adorno-commitment).

17   See Megan McLagan and Yates McKee (eds), 'Introduction', *Sensible Politics: The Visual Culture of Nongovernmental Activism*, Cambridge, Mass.: Zone Books, 2012, pp. 9-22.

example could be Trevor Paglen's (sometimes abstract or blurry) photographs of top-secret governmental, nuclear and military sites. Works such as Paglen's, seek to make visible the invisible under the premise that such an act is political. Yet, what images such as Paglen's represent is vague in political terms. What I find problematic is that the gap between *political* representation and *aesthetic* representation is now wider than ever. Representation means 'making the absent present', which is always an incomplete task because totality is impossible to convey, and it works in two senses. As *Vertreten* (or political representation) it means taking the place of others in order to speak on their behalf, and as *Darstellen* (or aesthetic representation) it is the form of representation that implies describing the other in the first person. Representation was brought into a crisis in the 1960s because it was accused of hiding the fact that the speaker was occupying the place of the represented and thus, workers and minorities were prompted to speak on their own behalf and in the first person. Nowadays, however, the gap between political (*Vertreten*) and aesthetic (*Darstellen*) representations is wider than ever. Whatever political acts encoded in medial forms may represent, they render it unstable, partly because politics have become unrepresentable due to a lack of stable political subjects; they are collective enunciations constantly 'becoming'. In this context, 'expressive' politics is valued over representation because 'it embodies rebellious subjectivities expressing themselves without delegation and they do so through formal and symbolic richness'.[18] One of the issues that rises is that there is lack of a common ground to universalize the multiplicity of singular struggles and social movements scattered across the world like archipelagos. There are just too many images in the infosphere, and 'sensible politics' exists for and by its own public, which is made up of social movements and politically minded cultural producers. In this regard, cultural infrastructure functions as the platform for 'sensible politics,' in which curators, museum directors and board members (sometimes representing corporate interests) select and contextualize artwork that presents certain events and social actions, thus determining the boundaries of public thinking.

Aside from its compensatory role, culture (when it is 'creativity' and cognitive production), is not only at the center of political action, but is also embedded in production and consumption processes, and in neoliberalism, at least insofar as it has thrived in post-Fordist (flexible) forms and conditions of labor. Neoliberalism has taken up the characteristics of aesthetic production. Signs and nascent meanings, desires and projections meet in the market because the post-Fordist economy is based on manufacturing experiences, signs and information. The core of the knowledge economy is creativity. This is why qualities of aesthetic production have become hegemonic and have transformed labor and consumption processes as well as aesthetic experiences. Not only sensations and feelings are trivialized and packaged for sale, disinterestedness (the core of aesthetic

---

18   Marcelo Espósito, 'Lecciones de historia. El arte, entre la experimentación institucional y las políticas del movimiento', SITAC 2009. http://marceloexposito.net/pdf/exposito_sitac.pdf (http://www.e-flux.com/journal/art-and-the-cultural-turn-farewell-to-committed-autonomous-art/).

experience as defined by Kant) has also vanished.[19] This arises as the result of aesthetic experience that is enslaved for profit, as well as subsumed to 'political' efficiency in the sense of State and corporate strategic investment in culture and the transformation of political action into sensible forms—as opposed to action. These tendencies are a result of what Stephen Shaviro describes as 'the ruthless cognition of aesthetic sensations and feelings', as they are transformed into data and exploited forms of labor which are marketed as fresh experiences, exciting lifestyle choices, or as socially-responsible cultural activities. In the political arena, thirty years of neoliberalism have crushed any confidence that we might have had in the social contract. If artists used to identify with the proletariat and social struggles, nowadays, aesthetic production—which is lacking a reflexive program in regards to the conditions of its own production—is geared just toward the supplementing of the entertainment market with cultivated and knowledge-able new experiences and sensations. Furthermore, through subsidizing art and cultural projects, corporations, states and arts patrons put into practice the following principle of the Prince Claus Fund: 'There can be no development without culture, and there can be no cultural development without freedom of debate'.[20] As this quote becomes evermore evident, the public expects from culture and art rigorous accountability, criti-cal questioning, democratic access, dialogue, openness and equal representation in the visual regime. This is posited as the road to development. In this context, culture is perceived as 'a basic need', as the founding principle of Prince Claus Fund states. Thus, states, corporations, the private sector and society attribute to art a decisive political, as they invest in culture with the purpose of generating political and economic surplus value. Bearing in mind that the autonomy of art is always a political matter, could art be politicized beyond its autonomy as a site for added value?

The condition of possibility of autonomous, committed art under the new neoliberal world order, is radically different from what we see as the autonomy of art under mod-ernism (as *l'art pour l'art*) and post-modern interdisciplinarity. These imply the institu-tionalization of the avant-garde and the subsumption of art to the market, bearing in mind that the emancipatory promises of modernism (criticality, self-design, creativity) are now located at the center of our everyday lives both via consumption and production processes. Theodor Adorno's take on the autonomy of art in his 1962 essay entitled *Com-mitment,* can be helpful here. In this essay, Adorno responds to Jean-Paul Sartre's aes-thetic manifesto *What is Literature?* and elaborates a theoretical debate about engaged literature and autonomous art. According to Adorno there are two kinds artworks. On the

---

19   Stephen Shaviro, 'Accelerationist Aesthetics,' *e-flux journal* #46 (Summer 2013).

20   From their website: "... The Prince Claus Fund's mission is to actively seek cultural collaborations founded on equality and trust, with partners of excellence, in spaces where resources and opportunities for cultural expression, creative production and research are limited and cultural heritage is threatened. The Prince Claus Fund is based in Amsterdam and is supported by the Dutch Ministry of Foreign Affairs and the Dutch Postcode Lottery." For more information, visit their website: http://www.princeclausfund.org/en/the-fund.

one hand, there are works that 'are vulgarly assimilated to the existence against which they protest'.[21] These works 'are content with being mere fetishes or a pastime, and thus degenerate and become de-politicized cultural merchandise'.[22] This de-politicization, for Adorno is in fact, deeply political. A lot of politically or socially-minded contemporary art would fit into this category. On the other hand, there is *engaged autonomous art* which is necessarily detached from reality. Adorno defines the autonomy of art not in the sense of its strictly formalist aspect, although like Walter Benjamin, Adorno also vouches for works of art that are both formally and politically progressive. For Adorno, autonomous art negates a direct connection to reality. The distance that autonomous art has from reality, however, is mediated by reality itself. This means that a work of art cannot come out of the blue: its origin is a reaction against reality. Adorno, as does Benjamin, draws a distinction between 'commitment' and 'tendency'. Committed art does not bear the intention of generating betterment measures, legislative acts, practical institutions (like propaganda) or even transmitting a concrete ideology. It operates at the level of fundamental attitudes. For Adorno, autonomous and engaged works of art operate at the level of abandoning the social contract with reality and 'cease to speak as if they were reporting the facts: this is the moment in which a work of art makes people's hair stand up'.[23] According to Adorno, the shock of the unintelligible (or the ambiguous), is able to communicate more than what is legible and explicit. In that sense, works of art are autonomous, instead of heteronomous. Heteronomy implies that an artwork is subject to a different power, a law that is external and foreign to art and its formal logic. When it is autonomous, engaged art is neither subject to empirical reality nor a correct political tendency. Art's autonomy protects it from popularization and adoption by the market. Its autonomy implies liberating it from any other external purpose: from being useful. In this manner, an autonomous work of art does not convey a message nor does it need to convince the public or preach to the converted. And although it opposes society, autonomous art is still part of it.

If the autonomy of modern art implied considering art as a realm distanced from reality, art's post-medium condition now means that it has become a niche within reality.[24] What is at stake in autonomous art nowadays, would be to posit it as an experience of reality that is fundamentally foreign and antagonistic to the prevailing reality. If the autonomy

---

21   Theodor Adorno, 'Comittment', *New Left Review* I/87088 (September-December 1974), http://newleftreview.org/I/87-88/theodor-adorno-commitment (http://whitney.org/file_columns/0002/9848/andreafraser_1_2012whitneybiennial.pdf).

22   Adorno, 'Comittment'.

23   Adorno, 'Comittment'.

24   Marina Vishmidt, 'Mimesis of the Hardened and Alienated: Social Practice as a Business Model,' *e-flux journal* 43 (March, 2013), http://www.e-flux.com/journal/"mimesis-of-the-hardened-and-alienated"-social-practice-as-business-model (http://eipcp.net/transversal/0102/marchart/en).

of art should be located in the realm of reproduction, as Marina Vischmidt argues,[25] it would oppose the realm of production of the social, political and economic surplus value. It would go against embodying power and the entrepreneurial model of work. Producing difference and dragging out the laboring conditions hidden within it, autonomous art would imply mimesis with distancing itself. Beyond being used as a tool, autonomous art would refuse becoming an instrument against its own illusions, as well as refusing to become a political force, to be subjected to interests foreign to itself or simply becoming a pleasing commodity. Overcoming self-censorship, it would cease to participate in the economy of the globalized art world, especially in the name of critical practices, political work or social justice, abandoning its claim to become a progressive social force.[26] Above all, it would work against the power of culture and the culture of power.

References

Adorno, Theodor. 'Commitment', *New Left Review* I (87088) (September-December, 1974), http://newleftreview.org/I/87-88/theodor-adorno-commitment.

Emmelhainz, Irmgard. 'Art and the Cultural Turn: Farewell to Committed Autonomous Art?', *e-flux journal* 42 (February, 2013), http://www.e-flux.com/journal/art-and-the-cultural-turn-farewell-to-committed-autonomous-art.

Espósito, Marcelo. 'Lecciones de historia. El arte, entre la experimentación institucional y las políticas del movimiento', 2009. SITAC lecture, http://marceloexposito.net/pdf/exposito_sitac.pdf.

Foster, Hal. 'What's Neo about the Neo-Avant-Garde?', *October*, Vol. 70 (Autumn, 1994): 5-32.

Fraser, Andrea. 'Le 1% c'est moi', 2011, http://whitney.org/file_columns/0002/9848/andreafraser_1_2012whitneybiennial.pdf.

Marchart, Oliver. 'Art, Space and the Public Sphere(s)', 2002, http://eipcp.net/transversal/0102/marchart/en.

McLagan, Megan and McKee, Yates (eds). *Sensible Politics: The Visual Culture of Nongovernmental Activism*. Cambridge, Mass.: Zone Books, 2012.

Shaviro, Stephen. 'Accelerationist Aesthetics', *e-flux journal* #46 (Summer, 2013), http://www.e-flux.com/journal/accelerationist-aesthetics-necessary-inefficiency-in-times-of-real-subsumption.

Sholette, Gregory. 'Welcome to the Desert of the Real Artworld', *Oxford Art Journal* 27 (2) (2004) pp. 260-261. http://www.gregorysholette.com/wp-content/uploads/2011/04/07_welcome1.pdf.

Stakemeier, Kerstin and Vishmidt, Marina. 'The Value of Autonomy: A Conversation Between

---

25   Vishmidt, 'Mimesis of the Hardened and Alienated'.

26   Andrea Fraser, 'Le 1% c'est moi', 2011: 'Le gorille penseur est un guerrier: le guerrier est un être pour la mort, puisque son métier consiste à mourir. Ici, il pense un peu à la fin de son espèce, ou à la fin de l'ère des—notre époque n'est plus celle des guerriers, elle est celle des insectes, des animaux insignifiants, plus capables de s'adapter...' http://whitney.org/file_columns/0002/9848/andreafraser_1_2012whitneybiennial.pdf (http://www.e-flux.com/journal/accelerationist-aesthetics-necessary-inefficiency-in-times-of-real-subsumption/).

Kerstin Stakemeier and Marina Vishmidt About the Reproduction of Art', *Texte zur Kunst* 88 (December, 2012): 102-117.

Thompson, Nato. 2013, 'The Insurgents Part I: Community-Based Practice as Military Methodology,' *e-flux journal* # 47 (September, 2013), http://www.e-flux.com/journal/the-insurgents-part-i-community-based-practice-as-military-methodology.

Vishmidt, Marina. 'Mimesis of the Hardened and Alienated: Social Practice as a Business Model', *e-flux journal* # 46 (March, 2013), http://www.e-flux.com/journal/"mimesis-of-the-hardened-and-alienated"-social-practice-as-business-model.

Wu, Chin-tao. 'Embracing the Enterprise Culture: Art Institutions Since the 1980s', *New Left Review* I 230 (July-August, 1998).

Šefik Tatlić is a theorist from Bosnia-Herzegovina. He holds a PhD in sociology and his work focuses on political philosophy, decolonial theory and political sociology. Some of his recent publications include an essay 'The Emancipation of Necrocapitalism' (in Politics, Aesthetics and Democracy reader, Slovenian Academy of Arts and Sciences, Ljubljana, 2015) and a book entitled *The Logic of Humanization of Capital—Legitimization of Oppression and Devaluation of the Function of Political Power* (Orion Art, Belgrade, 2015). He is, with Marina Gržinić, co-author of the book *Necropolitics, Racialization and Global Capitalism: Historicization of Biopolitics and Forensics of Politics, Art, and Life* (Lexington Books, USA, 2014). He has been writing regulary for *Reartikulacija publication* (Ljubljana, Slovenia), published a lot of theoretical texts in various countries and gave a number of public lectures.

Gordana Nikolić is a curator and a theorist of contemporary art and media culture. She runs the Center for film, video and photography in the Museum of Contemporary Art Vojvodina, Novi Sad, Serbia. She has been involved with numerous projects including publishing, curating and lecturing in Serbia, United Kingdom, Netherlands, Slovenia, Croatia, Germany, Spain.
She co-edited the books *Artist at (non)work* (MCAV/kuda.org, Novi Sad, 2012, serbian) and *Free and Souvereign. Art, Theory and Politics.* (Cenzura, Novi Sad, 2013, english).
She also co-authored the project 'Technology to the People!' (2013), presenting around 150 art films and video experiments from the 20st Century in Vojvodina region. She co-curated recent exhibitions in 2014 and 2015 such as 'Absolutely Now: Death, Confusion, Sale', 'Archive and Power', and 'Jasmina Cibic: Building Desire'.

Sandi Abram is an independent researcher from Ljubljana, Slovenia who was graduated with a Bachelor in Social Informatics (Faculty of Social Sciences, Ljubljana) and a Master in Social and Cultural Anthropology (Faculty of Arts, Ljubljana). His research focuses on collective memory, reappropriations of public spaces, contemporary non-institutional practices of art, craft and artivism, and other forms of urban cultures. He is a member of the editorial board of the *Journal for the Critique of Science, Imagination, and New Anthropology*. He has published various essays on graffiti and street art, squatting, tattoos, contemporary illustration, creative industries, and urban politics.

Jonathan Beller is professor of Humanities and Media Studies and director of the Graduate Program in Media Studies at Pratt Institute. His books include *The Cinematic Mode of Production: Attention Economy and the Society of the Spectacle* (Dartmouth College Press, 2006) and *Acquiring Eyes: Philippine Visuality, Nationalist Struggle and the World-Media System* (Ateneo University Press, 2006). He serves on the editorial board of several journals, as *Social Text*, and is completing a book entitled *Computational Capital*.

Josephine Berry Slater is the editor of *Mute* magazine. She also teaches part-time at Goldsmiths on the Practices of the Culture Industry. Her current research interests are the transformation of public and community arts within the context of urban regeneration, and the urban politics of neoliberalism.

Irmgard Emmelhainz is an independent translator, writer and researcher based in Mexico City. In 2012, she published a collection of essays about art, culture, cinema and geopolitics, *Alotropías en la trinchera evanescente: estética y geopolítica en la era de la guerra total* (BUAP). Her work on topics related to movies, the Palestine Question, art, culture and, neoliberalism has been translated to German, Italian, Norwegian, French, English, Arabic, Turkish, Hebrew and Serbian. She is member of the editorial board of *Scapegoat Journal*, and her second book: *The Tyranny of Common Sense: Mexico's Neoliberal Conversion*, is forthcoming in Spanish.

Marc James Léger is an independent scholar living in Montreal. A longer version of his essay for *Gray Zones* is published as 'Gordard's Film Socialisme: The Agency of Art in the Unconscious' in his latest book, *Drive in Cinema: Essays on Film, Theory and Politics* (2015). He is the editor of *The Idea of the Avant Garde—And What It Means Today* (2014) and the author of *Brave New Avant Garde* (2012) and *The Neoliberal Undead* (2013).

Ana Vilenica is a researcher, theorist and activist. Graduated at Faculty of Philosophy in Belgrade and received her Ph.D. at the Department of Theory of Art and Media, University of Arts in Belgrade. She worked as a researcher in Academy of Arts in Novi Sad, investigating relations of urban regenerations, art and culture in local and regional context. She is the editor of the book *Becoming a mother in neoliberal capitalism* (uz)bu)) na))), Belgrade, 2013), co-editor of the book *On the Ruins of the Creative City* (kuda.org, Novi Sad, 2013), and the chief editor of *uz) bu))na)))* journal for art, politics, theory and activism (www.uzbuna.org). She regularly publishes texts on social issues in anthologies, journals, catalogs and portals. She is a member of the 'Who builds the city' initiative (www.kogradigrad.org).

www.ingramcontent.com/pod-product-compliance
Lightning Source LLC
Chambersburg PA
CBHW060639210326
41520CB00010B/1665